LIVE AT

SANTA MONICA'S LEGENDARY MUSIC VENUE

PETER ALAN LESSER

Published by The History Press
An imprint of Arcadia Publishing
Charleston, SC
www.historypress.com

Front cover: Michael Bloomfield. *Photo by Ellen Griffith.*
Back cover: George Thorogood (*left*) and John Hammond (*right*). *Photo by Gary Glade.*
McCabe's logo. *Courtesy McCabe's Guitar Shop.*
McCabe's Guitar Shop showroom. *Photo by Camila Wilson.*

First published 2026

Manufactured in the United States

ISBN 9781467159272

Library of Congress Control Number applied for.

CONTENTS

FOREWORD

By Bob Riskin, owner (retired), McCabe's Guitar Shop

The institution that today is called McCabe's Guitar Shop had its origins back in the late 1950s, when some friends in Los Angeles became interested in American and world folk music.

This is where we began. Gerry McCabe was a furniture designer and custom builder. He knew how to glue things, like guitars. He was in this circle of folk music enthusiasts, and they were always asking him for help. Perceiving that there was a need for a specialty store, he got together with Ed Kahn, a folklore student at University of California, Los Angeles (UCLA), who had connections to get Folkways Records releases and *Sing Out!* Magazines, and got some guitars to sell.

So it happened that on December 12, 1958, a small storefront opened for business on Pico Boulevard in Santa Monica. The sign read "Gerald L. McCabe, guitars banjos and mandolins." McCabe's was staffed mostly by part-timers and friends. It was open only a few hours each day. People would leave their instruments for repair, and Gerry would fix them in his furniture shop. The shop sold hand-woven straps, strings, and Mexican guitars.

When a Santa Monica College student, Walter L. Camp, became the first full-time employee and then a partner, it was called "McCabe & Camp." This often caused confusion. The public called us "McCabe's Guitar Shop," and eventually, we caved to the pressure and went with that as our business name.

Now it came to pass in 1959 or so, I became swept up in the urban folk music revival and became aware of McCabe's. It also happened that Walter

Camp frequently wanted to go get some lunch and would call me to cover for him. I worked summers and part time, finally settling into a full-time position in 1962.

The folk rock thing happened, and we were selling electrics and amps in addition to classical and steel string guitars. We had a house band, the Rising Sons. When Walter got tired of going east several nights a week to keep in touch with the music and the bands, we decided to bring the bands to us. Walter and I figured that if we had people in every week, we would be forced to clean up our work benches and the store generally. Later, we realized that the concert staff could do it!

We attracted musicians by actually paying them the night of the gig instead of just paying part or stalling. This unusual policy made our reputation in the business. We started doing concerts regularly in 1969 and haven't quit yet.

The last ingredient was there.

McCabe's was a place where you could buy instruments, learn to play them, have them fixed, buy books and recordings, and listen to performers.

All integrated under one roof.

Eventually, Gerry McCabe focused on his furniture business and sold his interest and Walter Camp moved to Mendocino. I ploughed on, shaping and guiding McCabe's to whatever the heck it is now.

I have described running McCabe's as the neatest job in the world.

Many would agree.

PREFACE

When I was conceiving the idea of writing the history of McCabe's Guitar Shop and its live concert series, two things became immediately evident. First, this was a story that definitely needed to be told. Second, there was no way that every event, group, or individual that contributed to the extraordinary history of this venue for over half a century could be included. With that in mind, the shop's tale is told through the recollections and reflections of just a few of the folks who have been a part of its story these many years, with the intention of providing the reader with a sense of the remarkable events and milestones that contributed to McCabe's Guitar Shop reputation as a legendary performance venue. I have tried to hit as many highlights as possible, and there is no doubt that there could easily be a second volume. Until then, here it is.

ACKNOWLEDGEMENTS

First and foremost, I want to express my deep appreciation to Kit Alderson for generously sharing his firsthand knowledge, enthusiasm, and copious files from decades of concerts at McCabe's Guitar Shop. Hardly a day went by that I didn't consult Kit or the materials he supplied for this book.

I would like to acknowledge—one by one—all the musicians, concert directors, music teachers, sound engineers, journalists, and artist managers who said *YES!* when asked to be interviewed for this project and for taking the time to reach back and share their memories. I'd also like to thank each photographer who graciously contributed their images to illustrate this story. Alas, space does not allow for individual thanks, but they are all named throughout these pages.

Thank you to Arcadia Publishing and The History Press acquisitions editor Laurie Krill for her support and advice throughout the process, and copy editor Ashley Hill for kindly bringing this project to the finish line.

Loving gratitude to my wife, Therese, and daughters, Corrina and Lillian, for their proofreading, diplomatic guidance in offering suggestions for improvements, and decades of support as I have pursued my passion for live music.

1
FOUNDING FATHERS

Gerald McCabe was not a musician or an experienced entrepreneur, but in 1958, he founded one of America's longest-surviving music stores that also became the home of a renowned concert series. It has featured many of the world's foremost American roots musicians since 1969.

"Business was not Dad's strong suit," admits Molly McCabe, the youngest daughter of Gerald McCabe. "But he did know when the time was right to open a guitar shop."

An extraordinarily skilled craftsman who would go on to become a highly regarded designer and builder of mid-century furniture, Gerald "Gerry" McCabe was born in Long Beach, California, in 1927. He served in the Navy during World War II and earned a bachelor's degree at the University of California, Los Angeles (UCLA), and a master's degree at California State University, Long Beach, both in fine arts.

While taking a folk music class at UCLA, Gerry met Marcia Berman, a Los Angeles native who was working toward her degree in education in preparation for a career as an elementary and preschool teacher. Gerry and Marcia soon started dating. They got married in 1956 and welcomed their daughter Hally later that year. The young family moved to Santa Monica, a city on the Pacific coast, fifteen miles west of Los Angeles, and settled into Pico Place, an enclave inhabited by musicians, visual artists, writers, and educators.

"My mom was running with a crowd that was into folk music, and she was a folk musician," explained Hally McCabe. On occasion, Pico Place

Gerald McCabe and his daughter Hally. *Photo provided by Hally McCabe.*

was cordoned off to accommodate the informal gatherings of live music organized by Marcia and her friends who were passing through Los Angeles on tour. Participants in these "hootenannies" included the likes of folk music heroes Odetta, Frank Hamilton, Ronnie Gilbert, and the Seegers, Pete, Peggy, and Mike.

The musicians would not just come to play. "My dad just loved working with wood…and people started bringing their guitars to my Dad to fix," remembered Hally. The word was out, and the guitars started piling up in Gerry's furniture studio.

To meet the increased need for repairs and seeing the demand for the sale of new guitars, Gerry opened his first guitar shop in a small storefront at 3015 Pico Boulevard in Santa Monica on December 12, 1958, the same year the Kingston Trio topped the pop chart with "Tom Dooley" and the folk boom became an explosion.

When asked if her dad saw guitar repair as a lucrative business, Hally reflected, "My dad was never motivated by money. He just had the skills, and he always liked the challenge of working with wood. I think he started it more as a service."

To stock the shelves, Gerry would travel to Paracho, the Mexican guitar capital, and bring back instruments to sell at the store. Then Gerry asked his friend Ed Kahn, a graduate student in ethnomusicology at UCLA whose acquaintances included prominent folk music historian Alan Lomax and legendary troubadour Woody Guthrie, to open a record and book concession at the newly opened shop. Ed had the connections to Folkways Records, founded by Moses Asch in 1948 to document "the people's music," spoken word pieces, instruction, and sounds from around the world, and the quarterly folk music bible *Sing Out!* magazine to sell at the store. He also decorated the shop's walls with banjos and exotic instruments borrowed from his friend and musician Guy Carawan, the director at the Highlander Research and Education Center, at the time known as the Highlander Folk School, a social justice leadership training school and cultural center in New Market, Tennessee.

Meanwhile, over in Malibu, the beach town just north of Santa Monica, eighteen-year-old college student Walter Camp was working at Positano's, a bohemian-style coffee shop where local musicians would sing and play guitar. Walter soon began befriending many of the performers who turned him on to folk music, and he was eventually introduced to Marcia Berman and Gerry McCabe. Once they became better acquainted, the store owner convinced Walter to leave the coffeehouse to become the first full-time employee of McCabe's Guitar Shop.

As Gerry's apprentice, Walter quickly learned the craft of guitar repair, freeing up the store owner to concentrate on his furniture design projects in his studio in Venice, the community just south of Santa Monica. In time, many of Ed Kahn and Marcia Berman's folk music friends began checking out the store, and with a variety of instruments to try and free coffee available, pop-in visits turned into longer stays and, ultimately, extended jam sessions.

While McCabe's was a busy hangout for both local and traveling musicians, its income from repairs and instrument, book, and record sales was not enough to make ends meet, and by 1960, Walter Camp was owed a substantial amount of back pay. Instead of taking out a loan—and in an effort to retain Walter as an employee—Gerry proposed to replace the debt by offering Walter 50 percent ownership of McCabe's Guitar Shop. Walter accepted.

Around this time, sixteen-year-old Robert "Bob" Riskin stopped in the store and purchased a couple of banjo instruction books. He recalled finding McCabe's "low-key, friendly and happening," and he kept returning. Before long, he was helping out by sweeping the floor, preparing hand mailings, and performing other odd jobs. He would also mind the store when Walter took his lunch break, and he spent his first summer at the shop fixing his own hand-me-down guitar.

Above: Walter Camp in the store, circa 1964 (notice the "Ringo for President" poster). *Photo by Bob Riskin.*

Left: Bob Riskin with a Martin guitar. *Photo by Dave Zeitlin.*

Bob Riskin became intrigued by all aspects of the business, including bookkeeping, which was never Walter or Gerry's strong suit. Young Bob organized the store's books, and once he successfully avoided the draft, he was hired as a full-time employee.

In an effort to reach wannabe musicians beyond their Santa Monica storefront, McCabe's opened branches at two legendary Los Angeles folk music venues: the Ash Grove and the Troubadour. Walter Camp also opened a McCabe's Guitar Shop in Long Beach, California, but it was not officially affiliated with the Santa Monica store.

Acoustic guitar sales got another boost in the early 1960s with folk song interpreters, such as Joan Baez and Peter, Paul and Mary, garnering national attention, and this was subsequently reinforced with the emergence of the singer-songwriter movement led by Bob Dylan. As a result, McCabe's was picking up steam and running out of room, so in 1964, it moved down the road to 3103 Pico Boulevard, a 1,500-square-foot store that had room for a classroom, an office, and a studio in the back.

McCabe's timed its move to a larger space perfectly, as 1964's British music invasion had customers seeking electric guitars and basses. It now had room to accommodate this new inventory along with the legions of local musicians and performers touring through Los Angeles who would stop by for the free coffee and to see who else might be hanging around in the front room in need of a picking partner.

2
RISING SONS

"I have no children, but I have sons," proclaimed legendary blues guitarist and gospel singer Reverend Gary Davis. He was at a New York City concert performed by guitarist David Bromberg, who had recently spent time leading the blind musician in exchange for an opportunity to take lessons from the fingerpicking virtuoso. Other disciples who had the exceptional opportunity to learn from this blues legend included Stefan Grossman, Steve Katz, Roy Bookbinder, Dave Van Ronk, Rory Block, Larry Campbell, Woody Mann, and Bob Weir, to name a few.

In Los Angeles, it was Stephen Nicholas Gerlach, better known as Jesse Lee Kincaid, who, in addition to being one of the Reverend's "sons," was also a nephew—his uncle was twelve-string guitar master Fred Gerlach.

Jesse first heard the sounds of the twelve-string floating through his apartment as a young boy when his uncle paid a visit to his Los Angeles home. He played songs from his recent recording *Gallows Pole and Other Folk Songs* on the Audio-Video record label (later rereleased as the album *Twelve String Guitar* on Folkways Records). Jesse was intrigued, and Fred gave him a six-string guitar as well as a few rudimentary lessons, and the teenager spent the next few years learning folk standards and perfecting the songs on his uncle's album.

Jesse also discovered McCabe's Guitar Shop, both the Ash Grove location, where he became friendly with Kenny Edwards who was then working behind the counter and who would soon become a member of the band the Stone Poneys, and the Santa Monica store, where he purchased a Gretsch guitar and first heard the name Ry Cooder.

Born and raised in Santa Monica, Ryland Peter "Ry" Cooder first became fascinated with roots music before he even entered the first grade. A friend of his mother had some 78-RPMs by the folk music icon Leadbelly that caught the boy's attention, and the same man gave Ry his first guitar and encouraged him to learn to play.

In an interview at the Country Music Hall of Fame in Nashville, Ry recalled that, as an elementary school student, he would split his time listening to and learning to play along with the songs on the local country music radio station and Woody Guthrie recordings. His mailman happened to be Ed Kahn, the ethnomusicologist who managed the record and sheet music department when McCabe's Guitar Shop first opened its doors. Along with the letters and packages on his mail truck, Ed kept a box of record albums to be delivered to area music stores. Ry would often ride along on Ed's route, thumbing through the albums, which helped to broaden his awareness of other artists who would influence the young musician, such as Joseph Spence, who had a major effect on the budding guitarist. It wasn't long before he discovered McCabe's Guitar Shop.

In a 2010 *Los Angeles Times* article, Ry remembered that instead of taking him home after school, the bus would drop him off at McCabe's, where he would wait to see who would come through the door. It was there that he first encountered the bluegrass musicians Roland and Clarence White. He

The Country Boys in 1960, with a young Clarence White, before they became the Kentucky Colonels. *Photo by Bob Riskin.*

recounted that it was fascinating for him to see people sit down a couple of feet away and play something really good that he wanted to learn.

In an interview on radio station KCRW, Walter Camp recounted that Ry became obsessed with the guitar and remained in the store throughout the afternoon until his parents arrived to take him home for supper. It wasn't long before Ry mastered the instrument, and soon, others would come by the shop just to listen to *him* play. When someone was befuddled about how different guitarists played certain licks, McCabe's staff would play the recordings in question for Ry. He would listen, and typically, by the third time through, he would be playing along—mysteries solved.

In the *Los Angeles Times* interview, Ry went on to say that without McCabe's Guitar Shop, he might not have learned to play the guitar as quickly as he did. Otherwise, he may have been working at a grocery store or delivering pizza for a living.

Jesse Lee Kincaid recalled, "People were saying 'Ry Cooder! You have to hear Ry Cooder!'" Jesse wanted to see what all the fuss was about, and he went to see the young musician perform in a concert where he was backing up the singer/songwriter Pamela Polland at the Ash Grove. The two

Ry Cooder at McCabe's, circa 1964. *Photo by Bob Riskin.*

guitarists became acquainted, and subsequently, Ry began giving lessons to Jesse, sharing his knowledge of the styles of ragtime blues players like Blind Blake and Blind Boy Fuller. However, the lessons did not last very long, as Ry told Jesse, "I'm not going to teach you anymore because you are learning everything I got."

Jesse went back to teaching himself, trying now to sort out the complexities of Reverend Gary Davis's picking style, and when he heard that the guitarist was doing a run of shows at the Ash Grove in 1964, he decided to go. He arrived early and found the Reverend just hanging around the venue, since he did not have any accommodations booked. "So, I thought, 'Oh well, I'll bring him home with me.'"

For the next two weeks, Jesse became the blind musician's liaison, taking him to the gigs he had booked in the area. "We would stay up pretty late at night, and he was showing me how to play his stuff."

As the Reverend prepared to depart Los Angeles, he invited Jesse to come stay with him in New York. The young musician jumped at the chance to continue learning from the guitar master and soon found himself driving across the country. While the valuable lessons continued, Jesse spent the lion's share of his time escorting Reverend and Mrs. Davis around the city for their various appointments. "It was getting fairly mundane at that point," Jesse recalled. While waiting for the Reverend to finish performing at a folk festival in Amherst, Massachusetts, Jesse became acquainted with a family who invited him to come to Cambridge, a city near Boston in the eastern part of the state, to check out the thriving folk music scene there. Jesse accepted, and upon his arrival, one of his first stops was the city's famous folk coffee house, Club 47 (now known as Club Passim). It was there that he first saw and heard Taj Mahal.

Born Henry Saint Clare Fredericks Jr. in New York City and raised in western Massachusetts, Fredericks's moniker Taj Mahal came to him in a dream, and he started using the stage name as the lead singer of the rhythm and blues band, the Elektras. Taj attended an agricultural college before he chose a career as a musician and moved to Cambridge.

Taj recalled the day he met Jesse: "I was running the open mic hootenanny night at Club 47, and I put him on stage and told him he had two songs. People liked him, so he did one more for an encore. He had great songs, and he had great respect for the music he was playing."

As it turned out, Jesse ended up renting a room in the same house Taj was living in, and inevitably, the two started playing together. Consequently, Taj invited Jesse to accompany him on some gigs he had booked on the

East Coast. While Jesse was still predominantly performing his Uncle Fred's arrangements on the twelve-string guitar in his Cambridge performances, it was when he picked up a six string that he really captured Taj's attention.

"He started playing some Blind Blake and Reverend Gary Davis kind of stuff. Then he really got into Blind Boy Fuller. So, I asked him, 'Hey man, where did you learn to play like that?' He said, 'Well, you know, I took some lessons from this guy out in California named Ry.' And I said, 'Really? Do you think that guy would like to be in a band? Could we get him out here?'

Jesse responded, "Well I don't know, he's seventeen years old."

And Taj said, "Seventeen years old? Then we're going to California!"

Taj asked his agent, Manny Greenhill from Folklore Productions, to book them some gigs as they worked their way west, with a final show in Detroit, where Jesse had some family. The plan was to then hitchhike to California, but instead, they found a family who needed their car driven across country. It was a brand-new 1965 Cadillac Coup de Ville. "So, we came out to California in style. All we had to do was pay for the gas and make sure we didn't scratch it up," Taj recalled.

After delivering the car to northern California, Taj and Jesse hitchhiked to Berkeley and busked on the city streets until they got enough money to get to Los Angeles, where they stayed in the backyard shed at Jesse's parents' house.

Within a few days, Taj met and played with Ry Cooder and became acquainted with McCabe's Guitar Shop. "It was the place where things were happening," Taj recalled.

Taj also spent a fair amount of time at the Ash Grove. "Taj lived at the Ash Grove—literally—he was our unpaid night watchman," remembered Mary Katherine Aldin, who worked as an assistant to club owner Ed Pearl from 1962 to 1972. "There was a little area upstairs by the sound booth. Many an afternoon when I was in my office, I could hear Taj in the front room teaching himself how to play piano." Taj eventually decided to settle in Santa Monica and rented an apartment on 21st Street and Pico Boulevard, about ten blocks from McCabe's.

Taj and Jesse were soon booked to play at the Ash Grove, and Ry Cooder attended the show. After the concert, Ry told them that the folks at McCabe's Guitar Shop had rented a booth at the 1965 Teenage Fair at the Hollywood Palladium. The shop had asked him to represent them there, demonstrating Martin electric guitars, and he needed a band. Taj and Jesse agreed to join him, along with bassist Gary Marker and, eventually, drummer Ed Cassidy (who subsequently formed the rock band Spirit).

Left to right: Ry Cooder, Taj Mahal, Gary Marker, and Jesse Lee Kincaid at the Teenage Fair. *Photo by Bob Riskin.*

Taj remembered the experience well: "We were the guys playing the electric guitars…having a great time, you know, just jamming on old blues stuff."

After five days of playing together, they walked out as a new band: the Rising Sons. McCabe's co-owner Walter Camp initially signed on as the group's manager, and they would often practice at his house near the beach.

Taj and Jesse booked some dates at the New Balladeer, a folk club in west Los Angeles, and they were soon joined by the rest of the band. The full group was later engaged by the Ash Grove for a ten-night run. Then things really started moving quickly. The William Morris Agency started booking them up and down the Sunset Strip, and they signed a recording contract with Columbia. However, when the band's first single failed to chart, the label decided not to release their self-titled album and dropped them. After floating around for decades on bootleg albums, the recording was eventually released on compact disc in 1992.

Subsequently, Jesse Lee Kincaid went to music school to study classical guitar, signed a songwriting contract with MGM, released some music on Capitol Records, and then moved to Europe. Upon his return, Jesse settled in Northern California. His 2014 album, *Brief Moments, Full Measure,* features some tracks with Taj on banjo and harmonica.

While the Sons' career set just as quickly as it had risen, it was the catalyst for the extraordinarily successful and highly awarded careers of Taj Mahal and Ry Cooder, with each going on to record dozens of blues, folk, jazz, and world music albums and score multiple movie soundtracks. Between them, they have been nominated for over thirty Grammys and have received a dozen awards, including a mutual win when they reunited in 2022 to record the Sonny Terry and Brownie McGhee tribute album *Get on Board.*

3

WALK RIGHT IN

Taj Mahal remained in Santa Monica until 1970, often visiting McCabe's Guitar Shop to check out the guitars and stock up on picks, strings, and capos. "It was like a moveable feast. You never knew who you would run into. I saw everyone from Johnny Cash to Tuesday Weld in that place."

Then one night, in walked the Munsters. Taj recalled hanging out at McCabe's Ash Grove store when Herman (Fred Gwynne) and Grandpa (Al Lewis), of the 1960s sitcom *The Munsters* fame, came in after a concert by Lightnin' Hopkins.

"Fred was looking at the albums, and whatever he picked up, Al said to Fred, 'No, no, no—this one…Bukka White! Son House!…*This* is the real music.'" Sure enough, Fred put down the album he was considering and went with Al's suggestions.

McCabe's wasn't the only Santa Monica store frequented by Taj Mahal. "On Ocean Avenue, there was little head shop that used to be there, and that was literally the first place I heard any of my music being played outside of the recording studio." He returned to the shop quite often and many times found that his self-titled debut LP on Columbia Records was in rotation.

Taj also spent much of his free time fishing off the Santa Monica and Venice Piers. "My whole interest in saltwater fishing started out there," he recalled. "McCabe's always kept me connected to a wide swath of music that was not the usual fare that everyone was listening to."

One day in 1966, Esperanza "Espie" Santa Cruz walked into McCabe's to shop for a new guitar. While Gerry McCabe was not spending much time at his namesake shop, he happened to be there working alone that day. However, he needed to leave for a moment to photograph one of his furniture pieces at his studio. With Walt and Bob out of the shop, he asked Espie if she could mind the store for a moment. He showed her how to operate the cash register and left her there alone. Before long, Bob returned, only slightly surprised to see a customer minding the shop. He ended up selling Espie an Amezcua Guitarra, one of the guitars McCabe's imported from Mexico.

So began one of the many courtships started at McCabe's Guitar Shop, and Bob and Espie were married a year later. Espie's initial introduction to the cash register was not gone for naught, as she eventually became head of business operations after a career in the biotech industry. She still has the guitar she bought at McCabe's that day in 1966.

The founding fathers of McCabe's were ever resourceful and always looking for a better way to serve their customers. Finding that the instruments they were bringing up from Mexico were prone to cracking, McCabe's became partners in a company that imported Japanese Zen-On guitars. They also introduced D'Addario Strings to the West Coast, with the company making the highly superior brass-wound strings to the exact specifications recommended by McCabe's.

At the time, there weren't any resource materials or standard methods for guitar maintenance and repair, so the McCabe's team often had to devise their own. Bob Riskin recalled building string winders, a tool that makes restringing a guitar easier and faster.

In 1962, McCabe's began constructing custom Appalachian dulcimers, but production lapsed when the company's chief builder, Mike Marcus, left to go to law school. In 1969, Bob Riskin decided to completely redesign the mold, resulting in a superior instrument. Employee Carmi Simon subsequently took Bob's design, formed a partnership with McCabe's, and started the Dulcimer Works down the road on Olympic Boulevard, eventually building over one thousand instruments from 1968 to 1975.

The twelve-string guitar was primarily considered a novelty instrument in the early part of the twentieth century, although it gained some respect in the hands of blues legends like Leadbelly and Blind Willie McTell in the 1920s, and Pete Seeger famously played and published instruction books on the instrument. In fact, Jesse Lee Kincaid's uncle Fred Gerlach found it so difficult to find a twelve-string in the 1950s that he started to make the instruments himself.

When the Rooftop Singers hit the pop charts in 1963 with their twelve-string-accompanied smash "Walk Right In," the demand for the instrument surged. McCabe's had a few Mexican and Gibson twelve-strings, but that

Walter Camp with a McCabe's dulcimer. *Photo by Bob Riskin.*

was not enough to go around. No problem for the ever-inventive duo of Walter Camp and Bob Riskin, who calculated that if they took a Martin 0021 guitar, the only model with a wide neck, and spliced on a lengthened peghead and new bridge, they could transform it to a twelve-stringer. Of course, it worked beautifully, and sales were off and running. Martin was consequently inundated with requests for the instruments and started their production on its own.

While McCabe's never built guitars itself, Jack MacKenzie, who repaired instruments in the 1970s, said that Japanese guitar designers occasionally consulted with the staff at McCabe's. "I recall the Yamaha people bringing a couple of prototype capos into the shop for our opinion on them. There was something of a language barrier to our interaction, and when one of them handed me a capo, I put it in my pocket and said, 'Thank you.' Being honorable and polite in full Japanese tradition, they never asked for it back. A touch heavy by modern standards, but very durable and functional—I still have it."

In 1974, Bob Taylor and Kurt Listug came in searching for a Los Angeles store to sell the guitars they were making by hand. McCabe's team gave them a listen and offered to take the three guitars they had brought with them, but they did suggest that it would be beneficial to have more clarity in the treble strings. Bob and Kurt took the advice to heart, and when they returned with their next batch of instruments, the clarity was there. It is the tone that exemplifies Taylor guitars, which went on to be sold through hundreds of retail locations in North America, with international distribution to sixty countries. McCabe's Guitar Shop was Taylor Guitars' first dealer.

Then in the 1980s, Bob Riskin called Taylor Guitars and asked if there was anything unique the company wanted to try. At the time, Taylor designer Larry Breedlove had become fascinated by a wood furniture painting technique he was anxious to try on a guitar. Taylor produced one of these painted guitars. McCabe's liked it, and subsequently, the Taylor "Artist Series" was born. They were soon in the hands of countless guitarists, including Prince and Kenny Loggins.

4
PREMIERE PERFORMANCES

Mike Seeger, a member of the traditional folk music trio the New Lost City Ramblers, was a friend of McCabe's dating back to the hootenanny days on Pico Place that jump-started the opening of the shop. He would stop in the store when on tour through Los Angeles, and on one particular visit, he added a new dimension to the future of McCabe's Guitar Shop.

Elizabeth "Libba" Cotten taught herself to play guitar as a young girl growing up in North Carolina. She was a leftie and turned a right-handed guitar upside down when she played. Before long, she was writing her own songs, including "Freight Train," which would go on to become a standard of the folk music repertoire. Once Libba married and had a family, she stopped playing until she was hired as a housekeeper for Mike Seeger's family. Being surrounded by folk music, Libba picked up the guitar again, and with Mike's encouragement, she recorded her first album in 1960 on Folkways Records.

Libba and Mike subsequently began to tour the country together, and in February 1969, they were scheduled to perform a concert at Royce Hall on the UCLA campus. However, when they arrived, they found that the show had been canceled, leaving the duo without sufficient funds to return home to the East Coast. Mike then went to McCabe's and asked his friends Walter Camp and Bob Riskin if they had any suggestions of a way they could earn the money they needed to get back home.

They did—they offered McCabe's Guitar Shop as a substitute concert venue for the duo. With the performance only two days away, there was

Left to right: Walter Camp, Elizabeth Cotten, and Mike Seeger at the first "Live at McCabe's Guitar Shop" performance. *Photo by Bob Riskin.*

not much time to spread the word, but Walter and Bob got on the phones and, sure enough, on the night of February 23, 1969, people were lined up outside the storefront to see the show. With the shop windows covered (to hide the gathering from public view, as the store did not have a permit to present live music), Mike and Libba performed on a makeshift stage, the first concert at McCabe's Guitar Shop.

Three weeks later, another stranded musician came to McCabe's. Inspired by folk music legend Woody Guthrie, Ramblin' Jack Elliott began touring the land in the 1950s and became familiar with McCabe's while traveling through Los Angeles. On this occasion, Jack's transmission decided its own rambling days were over, and when he explained the situation to his friends at McCabe's, they knew just what to do to raise the cash he needed to fix the car. For two nights, March 17 and March 18, 1969, Jack regaled the audience with songs and stories from atop the guitar repair workbenches. On the second night, Arlo Guthrie, the son of Woody who had come to national prominence in 1967 with the eighteen-plus-minute story song "Alice's Restaurant" that comprised the entirety of side one of his debut LP, was in town recording his *Runnin' Down the Road* album. He stopped by to join his friend on stage, and the place was packed for both shows.

In his concerts over the years, Arlo often quoted the famous line by comedian Charles Fleischer "If you remember the '60s you really weren't there," before telling the story of his appearance at the Woodstock music festival in August 1969 and launching into his classic song "Coming into Los Angeles." When asked about his guest appearance with Ramblin' Jack at McCabe's, Arlo proved the quote to be accurate, as he at first had no recollection of the event. Subsequently, while digging deeper, he reflected, "Anytime Jack was nearby, he'd stop in, as well as visa versa. We played together quite often and had fun doing it. I do remember something about Jack's transmission failing—I think he was driving a Land Rover or something exotic but can't be sure. It was a long time ago, and I didn't take notes hahaha."

The success of the two impromptu concerts reignited Walter Camp's longtime desire to start a concert series. The idea had been brewing since his days of hearing folk music at the Café Positano and his abbreviated stint as the manager of the Rising Sons. On the other hand, Bob Riskin saw the possibility of a concert series as a practical way to keep the store clean. The guitar repair business generated a fair amount of sawdust, and by the end of each work week, it covered nearly every surface of the store. Transforming the shop into a concert venue would force the staff to get out the brooms and feather dusters to make the space presentable to both performers and audiences. Most importantly, Walter, Bob, and Gerry agreed that bringing people in for concerts had the potential to turn audience members into guitar customers as they perused the instruments that surrounded them.

The founding fathers also acknowledged that none of them had the time, connections, or experience to start producing concerts—but Walter Camp knew of someone who did.

In the early '60s, Robert "Bobby" Kimmel left his home in Tuscon, Arizona, for a California class in music at Santa Monica College. A singer, songwriter, guitarist, and bass player, Bobby soon became acquainted with fellow musician John "Kit" Alderson, who was in some of his music classes.

Kit Alderson recalled:

> *One day in 1964, a sort of different-looking guy wandered back and forth outside the Art Patio and eventually came over to talk. He told me he was "uptight" about bringing a great girl singer named Linda Ronstadt out from*

> *Tucson to form a band. He played me a few of his songs, all of which I thought were great.*
>
> *After a short time (months, I think), Bobby managed to persuade Linda to come out. I found out that Bobby, Linda, and Linda's boyfriend, Malcolm Terence, all lived in a small house on Hart Avenue near the beach in the Ocean Park neighborhood of Santa Monica. Bobby and Linda put a band together immediately, with Kenny Edwards on guitar and Stu Brotman on bass. For some reason, possibly having to do with differing musical tastes, Stu left the band after a very short time.*
>
> *At that point, Bobby brought Linda to the Art Patio to hear me play the autoharp, which I had just taken up the year before. When she heard me play, she said "I want him in the band."*
>
> *At our first rehearsal, Bobby Kimmel made us all get right down to business. Of course, this was when I met Kenny Edwards* [who was working at McCabe's at the Ash Grove location], *who immediately impressed me as a very intense and serious guy who also played some great guitar parts on Bobby's original songs. Bobby was more like a beatnik or hipster than anyone I had met at that time; his speech was full of phrases I had never heard, but it was entertaining. Linda was an enthusiastic and friendly young girl with an amazingly strong voice, and she was not shy about expressing her opinions about which songs or what kinds of music she wanted to do. By contrast, I was a shy guy who liked music a lot but was not as serious about the band as the rest of them. One of first things I remember Linda saying is that she liked Bobby because "he's got it covered on all levels."*

In an interview with *Rolling Stone* magazine, Linda recalled that they thought they were unique in the world—a quintet with an electric autoharp and a female singer—but it turned out the Lovin' Spoonful and the Jefferson Airplane had respectively beat them to it.

The band did get invited to record some songs in 1966, but the terms of the deal were concerning to some of the band members and they decided not to go forward. The band eventually broke up.

However, in the process, they did record four songs, two of which were released on 45-RPMs in 1968 on the Sidewalk label—"So Fine" and the Bobby Kimmel original "Every One Has His Own Ideas"—but they were immediately pulled from the market due to contractual considerations.

Before long, Bobby, Linda, and Kenny formed a folk trio, and like most area musicians, they spent some of their days at McCabe's Guitar Shop, where they got well acquainted with Walter and Bob. In 1966, they were discovered while rehearsing their vocal parts in a laundromat near the Hart Avenue house, and subsequently, they signed a recording contract with Capitol Records. The first Stone Poneys album came out in January 1967, and their follow-up album, which included the top ten hit single "Different Drum," brought them national acclaim.

While the band was able to ride on their initial success for a while, by the time they released their third album as Linda Ronstadt and the Stone Poneys—with Shep Cooke taking on the lead guitar duties for Kenny Edwards, who had departed—it was clear that Capitol Records' focus was on developing the lead singer as a solo artist.

Exhausted and discouraged, Bobby Kimmel was ready for a total change of scene, so he headed north up the California coast to Big Sur and the Esalen Institute. Founded in the early '60s with a vision to combine elements of Zen Buddhism, Western psychology, and Indian yoga into a decidedly utopian vision, Esalen was a far cry from the brutal realities of the commercial music industry.

Not long after, Walter Camp also made the trek north to Esalen—but not for a spiritual reawakening. Instead, he went to find Bobby Kimmel, who was serving as night watchman and tending the vegetable garden, to convince him to return to Santa Monica to manage a new concert series at McCabe's Guitar Shop.

As it turns out, Bobby was assessing his options for his next life chapter and thought he would open a small music venue somewhere in California. The invitation to be the founding director of a concert series at McCabe's Guitar Shop was a custom fit. Bobby Kimmel returned to Santa Monica.

5

BOBBY'S BLUES AND BLUEGRASS

Refreshed, reinvigorated, and ready to roll, Bobby Kimmel began working on the new concert series. He was also pumped to reignite his music career and quickly realized that he could kill two birds with one stone. Bobby's bandmate Kit Alderson from the first iteration of the Stone Poneys happened to be returning to town in November 1969 from Ithaca, New York, where he had been studying philosophy at Cornell University.

Kit recalled, "I drove to McCabe's to let people know I was back. Bobby Kimmel was there and told me that a new band was forming and that I was in it. That is how the Floating House Band started!"

The group, originally a quintet, opened many shows for the headliners at McCabe's. The group soon trimmed down to a trio of Bobby, Kit, and Shep Cooke, and they recorded a self-titled album on Takoma Records in 1971.

A flyer advertising the new series listed that on November 28–29, 1969, singer/songwriter Steve Gillette was scheduled to perform along with the Floating House Band, followed by a concert by Camp Hilltop and Mary McCaslin on December 5–6 and then a show by the Town & Country Boys on December 12–13.

It is unclear whether these events actually took place; however, photographs appear to indicate that the first "official" McCabe's concert was presented on December 19, 1969, headlined by the band Bryndle—Karla Bonoff, Kenny Edwards, Wendy Steiner (soon to be known as Wendy Waldman), and Andrew Gold—and the Floating House Band. Emerging singer/songwriter Jackson Browne was also a constant presence on stage

Nov 28 & 29
Steve Gillette
McCabe's Floating
House Band

Dec. 5 & 6
Camp Hilltop
and
Mary McCaslin

McCabe's Weekend Concerts
3103 Pico Blvd., Santa Monica
Shows at 8⁰⁰ & 10³⁰ $2.00 Admission
Sunday Night Hoots
Free Coffee and Cookies call 828-4497

Dec. 12 & 13: Bluegrass and Traditional Night

Dec. 19 & 20: Ken Edwards, Wendy Steiner, Andy Gold, Carla Bonoff
and McCabe's Floating House Band

Above: The first flyer for the "Live at McCabe's" concert series in 1969. *Courtesy of McCabe's Guitar Shop.*

Opposite: Bryndle on stage at McCabe's, December 19, 1969. *Left to right*: Kenny Edwards, Andrew Gold, Karla Bonoff, and Wendy Waldman. *Courtesy of McCabe's Guitar Shop.*

in those early years and, according to him—and McCabe's lore—was the opening act for that Bryndle concert.

The impromptu performances by troubadours Libba Cotten, Mike Seeger, Ramblin' Jack, and Arlo Guthrie perfectly symbolized McCabe's Guitar Shop's stature as the place to be during the folk boom of the 1950s and 1960s. As the official concert series kicked into high gear in the new decade, it was strategically positioned to take full advantage of the burgeoning singer-songwriter movement that was erupting in Los Angeles in the 1970s.

Jackson Browne was on stage at the new venue quite often, performing five concerts in 1970 alone.

Bobby Kimmel recalled that he booked Jackson as often as he could, because he knew that once his first album was released, he would no longer be able to touch him. Sure enough, when Jackson's long-awaited self-titled LP was released in 1972, including songs such as "Doctor My Eyes," "Rock Me on the Water," and "Jamaica Say You Will," his career skyrocketed, and he was soon headlining at the Troubadour a week at a time. However, Jackson never forgot the opportunity afforded to him by McCabe's as he road-tested his new songs, and he has returned to the stage on numerous special occasions.

The Floating House Band. *Left to right*: Bobby Kimmel, Kit Alderson, and Shep Cooke. *Photo provided by Kit Alderson.*

Bobby kept on the lookout for other promising Los Angeles–based artists, early on booking the band Longbranch/Pennywhistle, which featured future Eagle Glen Frey and J.D. Souther, who went on to a successful solo career and penned major hits for Linda Ronstadt, James Taylor, the Eagles and others. The duo of Mary McCaslin and Jim Ringer was a regular, and stage magician Ricky Jay often opened shows with his entertaining stories and card tricks. Later in his tenure as the concert director, Bobby presented a young Tom Waits at McCabe's.

One of the unspoken rules of thumb for concert presenters is "don't book your record collection," as oftentimes, the music you love may not necessarily be your audience's cup of tea. Many promoters have learned this lesson the hard way, as they can count on one hand the folks who have come to see their favorite artist.

Apparently, Bobby Kimmel did not heed this advice, but he must have had a great record collection because his taste in music was in fact in step with the folk music audience in Los Angeles. Bobby had a passion for blues and bluegrass and got right to work letting some of his heroes know that there was a new place to play in Los Angeles. Before long, the top touring acoustic blues musicians, including Mance Lipscomb, Sonny Terry & Brownie McGhee, and John Hammond, and bluegrass greats like Bill Monroe, the Dillards, and Byron Berline were playing live at McCabe's along with Jesse Lee Kinkaid's uncle Fred Gerlach, who had settled in Santa Monica.

Bobby also arranged for the return of Libba Cotten, Mike Seeger, and Ramblin' Jack Elliott, who were the catalysts of the Live at McCabe's series in 1969. Wayne Griffith, who went on to have a long career working concerts at McCabe's, recalls Ramblin' Jack's return: "I was working the door that night—7 p.m. rolls around, he's not here. He's supposed to do a sound check. The soundman is getting worried. At 8 p.m., [Jack's] big German Shepherd walks in the door, and about a minute later, Jack walks in, goes up on stage, and does a great show."

As impressive as the first year of performances was, the concert director's big break came in mid-1971, when he got a call from artist manager Manny Greenhill at Folklore Productions, which had recently opened shop in Santa Monica. He explained that one of the musicians on their roster was looking for a new place to perform in Los Angeles following an unpleasant experience at the Ash Grove. It was Doc Watson.

Arthel Lane "Doc" Watson was "discovered" in 1960 by folklorist Ralph Rinzler, who was on a field trip to record banjo picker Clarence "Tom" Ashley. Doc's extraordinary guitar skills, particularly his unique ability to flat-pick "fiddle tunes" with impeccable precision, and his treasure-trove of traditional tunes quickly earned him a recording contract and a coast-to-coast touring schedule. His son Merle started accompanying him in 1964, and by 1971, they were firmly established as American roots music royalty, playing major folk festivals, concert halls, and college campuses.

While Doc Watson was absolutely on Bobby Kimmel's booking bucket list, Bobby did not expect that the legendary musician would want to play such a tiny room after years of selling out the three-hundred-seat Ash Grove, yet Manny was on the line: "Doc Watson is looking for a gig. What can you pay him?"

Bobby had a solution: Doc and Merle Watson could play five nights at the shop. Of course, all the shows sold out, and, charmed by the intimacy of the venue, Doc made McCabe's his go-to performance place in Los Angeles for many years.

If seeing Doc Watson in such an intimate setting was a great treat for the audience, it was a real coup for the store's staff. Hally McCabe, who spent her childhood days playing with the cash register while her father was in the repair shop, started working at the store as a teenager and recalled what it was like when the legendary musician arrived with his entourage: "They would sit Doc down in the front room of McCabe's on the day of the concert.…He was glad to just stay there and play with whoever was there. So, we could play with or just watch Doc Watson close up. He was a delight!"

Mitch Greenhill, who started working with his father at Folklore Productions, was an accomplished guitarist who himself became a regular at McCabe's as a performer with his own bands and accompanying artists such as Paul Siebel and Rosalie Sorrels. He explained why Doc Watson returned time and again: "In general, artists enjoyed playing McCabe's. Attentive audience, good sound, and the artists were well treated. Doc was nostalgic for McCabe's."

6

WHEN THAT OLD GUITAR STARTS TO MAKE THAT SOUND

"Son, what's that sound?" Bobby Kimmel recalled Doc Watson asking this of Merle Watson at his first McCabe's sound check. Merle replied to his father, who was blind, "Well, Doc, there are guitars hanging on the wall." And Doc said, "Well, you gotta cover them up."

Longtime McCabe's sound engineer Alan Kanter had a solution. The most valuable guitars in the shop had little four-by-six-inch paper cardstock cards that read:

> *McCabe's Guitar Shop requests:*
> *REFRAIN FROM CLUTCHING TO BOSOM & holding, playing or scratching with fingernails and belt buckles*

Alan said, "I started getting those cards interwoven between every other string and placed over the sound hole, which drastically reduced the guitars' singing. Without the cards on the guitars, if you struck a note loudly enough and then abruptly stopped it, the room would sing for a good three seconds or more."

It wasn't the first time Alan's ingenuity came into play in the concert series. An extraordinarily focused, dyed-in-the-wool audiophile, Alan can remember the first time he attended a concert at the shop in the early '70s and can effortlessly recall the specifications of the equipment being utilized.

Who was performing?

I have no idea, but I walked into the door at McCabe's. They had set up card chairs, probably about thirty or forty of them. You simply walked in the door, and everything was right there. There was no stage to speak of; it was probably eight milk cases with plywood stacked on top of it and a couple of mic stands and a whole bunch of people milling about. The concert started. I don't know if it was a mistake on my part or not, but at intermission, when they set up the coffee and tea service in the back room, I went and talked to the person doing sound and I said, "You know it's really horrible sounding." They were using a pair of KLH, probably the model 6 or 5, bookshelf loud speakers—home hi-fi speakers—that were up high above the stage on a shelf, and a tiny little Kenwood integrated amplifier that couldn't have been more than about fifteen or twenty watts per channel, and the mic mixers were the only thing that I might call semi-pro; they were a pair of SONY Triple 7 mic mixers.

Alan explained to the person running sound, Kenny Moore, that the amplifier did not have nearly enough power and was therefore causing distortion. Moore responded, "Well, I'm not into that. I'm a cabinet maker." It turns out, they had rigged up the system on the fly for the first concert with Libba Cotten and Mike Seeger, and it remained in place. Alan suggested that they needed a more powerful amplifier to work with those speakers. Kenny politely noted that the budget for sound was zero.

While he knew what was needed to improve the sound, Alan was, at that time, a freshman studying electrical engineering at San Fernando Valley State College and was unable to provide anything more than advice.

As a fan of folk music, Alan continued to attend the occasional concert and became acquainted with Bob Riskin. He eventually helped design McCabe's first sound system. However, the shop did not have much pocket change to invest in the required equipment. By then, Alan was working at the Los Angeles hi-fi store Henry Radio (where he worked for fifty-two years) and was able to get parts at dealer cost. So, one piece at a time, a new and improved system was put in place. Eventually, Kenny Moore decided to hand over the sound mixing chores to Alan and Ron Marks.

Around this time, fourteen-year-old Wayne Griffith, whose sister Sue worked the concerts at McCabe's, came into the shop hoping to take banjo lessons, but he found that he could not afford to do so. But Wayne was resourceful, a trait which would come to benefit McCabe's Guitar Shop for over fifty years: "I swung a deal with Bobby Kimmel for me to come down before the concerts and help clean the place in exchange for banjo lessons."

Bobby agreed, and after helping transform the store into a concert venue each weekend, Wayne would stay to enjoy the shows. Recognizing Wayne's talent and work ethic, Bobby Kimmel officially hired him to become a member of the concert staff.

On the banjo, Wayne quickly graduated from taking beginner to intermediate lessons, and it wasn't long before he needed a better instrument. "I made my first banjo at McCabe's when I was sixteen, under the tutelage of Larry Brown, who was our guitar repairman," he said. Larry had learned the craft when he was working for luthier Ren Ferguson, who had a shop in Venice, California, before he moved on to work with legendary guitar makers Gibson, Fender, and Guild. Wayne became a fine craftsman himself and worked at Gerry McCabe's furniture shop as well as the Dulcimer Works. The stained-glass piece he created for McCabe's at age sixteen has been displayed at the store ever since.

When Wayne discovered that the person who did the sound mixing received twenty dollars a day—compared to the fifteen dollars made by the rest of the concert staff—he was inspired to learn that art at the age of seventeen. Wayne was always a quick study, and when soundman Ronnie Marks decided to move on, he became a full-fledged partner of Alan Kanter.

Wayne Griffith and his handmade stained-glass McCabe's sign. *Photo by Ellen Griffith.*

Eventually, he became the primary engineer for McCabe's. During the week, Wayne worked for documentary filmmaker Chuck Braverman Productions, ran the Barpassers Bar studio, and restored Vincent motorcycles. Then he went to McCabe's each weekend to man the sound booth.

Both Wayne and Alan enjoyed the challenges and rewards of mixing sound and recording concerts at McCabe's, always ensuring that they catered to the needs of the artist, taking extra care with microphone placement and finessing decibel levels, which could occasionally overpower the intimate performance space.

Woody Nuss, who has been behind the board at McCabe's since the early 1990s, recalled the first time he was charged with mixing sound for a concert by Odetta: "She was so awesome. I remember, I asked her, as soundmen do, 'Do you like this? Do you like that? And what about reverb? Is it okay to put reverb on your voice?' And she took a really long pause, and she looked at me square in the face, and said, 'If you could explain to me what reverb *is*, then you can use it.' So, the two of us had a long talk about reverb, why you use it, how it's applied. It was like an audio philosophy conversation with a legend." After a short pause, Odetta gave Woody the thumbs up. (Note: reverb, short for reverberation, is an electronically produced echo effect.)

Referring back to Doc and Merle Watson, Alan Kanter recalled that they initially performed acoustically, meaning they played their guitars into microphones. However, once the electric bassist T. Michael Coleman joined them, the father-and-son team began plugging their instruments into amplifiers. The volume caused some patrons to complain. Alan asked if the bassist might help lower the stage amplification. He tried, but just as Doc could hear the guitars on the wall singing, he could also sense immediately if his guitar amp had been adjusted, and he demanded it be restored to its original volume.

Alan reflected that, overall, audiences and artists rarely complained about the room's sound. "Musicians liked it, and there were no wait staff rambling around the tables saying, 'You haven't hit your two-drink minimum yet.' A lot of performers were very much intimidated the first time they played McCabe's because during intermission, they'll say things like, 'They're so damn quiet—they are paying attention.'"

Guitarist, singer, and songwriter Richard Thompson, who lived near McCabe's for a number of years and often went to concerts when he was not touring the world, recalled another time when the room's acoustics came into play. It was a concert by rhythm and blues "force of nature" vocalist

Etta James: "At one point, she put down the mic and just sang acoustically into the room over her pretty loud backing band, and you could still hear every word!"

Regarding the effect of the guitars on the wall, Richard recalled that when he played there, the cards were positioned on the strings to minimize the reverberation. "Before that, when the guitars were resonating, it must have been a great effect for some things (and some keys) but a nightmare if you didn't want it."

Guitarist Jorma Kaukonen, who first came to fame as lead guitarist for the psychedelic rock band the Jefferson Airplane, would bring his acoustic with him the many times he has played McCabe's, with bassist Jack Casady as Hot Tuna as well as with fiddler Papa John Creach, guitarist G.E. Smith, mandolinist Barry Mitterhoff, and multi-instrumentalist Larry Campbell. He added, "Everything in a listening room contributes to the environment....It would be hard to deny that all those stringed instruments are not going to resonate sympathetically and modify the listening experience."

In a statement in McCabe's fiftieth anniversary commemorative booklet, singer/songwriter Willie Nile said he considered the guitars on the wall as his bandmates: "The beautiful instruments on the wall seemed to be playing even with no one touching them. It was as if they were accompanying me that night. I swear I could hear them ringing."

Alternately, singer, songwriter, and guitarist Peter Rowan preferred to think of the guitars as additional audience members: "McCabe's is the neighborhood gig of dreams. All those instruments humming along as you sing and play! Magic!"

7
MOVING IN

Presenting Doc Watson elevated the concert series to new heights, giving McCabe's increased credibility with booking agents across the country. However, other things were happening that would even more significantly impact the guitar shop.

After basking in the glow of the launch of the concert series, Walter Camp was starting to become depressed. He had just broken up with his girlfriend, the store had recently been broken into, and he was having trouble making ends meet financially. Employees were starting to notice that he was behaving erratically. They were especially concerned when he started to come to the shop dressed in a dog suit. Bob Riskin recalled that the staff did not quite know how to respond. But guitar teacher Bob Baxter finally broke the ice by asking Walter, "May I help you, madam?"

That helped ease the tension that day, but soon thereafter, it all came to a head when the employees arrived to open the shop and found a guitar swinging from a noose. A stool had been kicked over beneath it, and there was a note from Walter that explained he was gone and would no longer be around. Walter Camp was done with the music business and had moved to Mendocino County in Northern California to find peace of mind.

While Walter was on a trajectory that led him to leave the shop and Gerald McCabe continued to spend the lion's share of his time designing furniture in his Venice studio, Bob Riskin was firmly in the driver's seat at McCabe's and became a partner in the business.

As the concert series began finding success, the work involved in transforming the showroom into a performance space with a portable stage each weekend, the expanding selection of musical instruments crowding the walls, and the constant flow of shoppers, music students, and ticket buyers was seriously cramping the style of McCabe's. With this in mind, Bob Riskin kept his eye on the two-story, four-thousand-square-foot space next to the shop, four times the size of the current location. As early as 1970, Bob started envisioning what could happen at 3101 Pico Boulevard—an expanded showroom and workshop, studios for music lessons, dressing rooms for show nights, and a space for concerts with a permanent stage and increased seating capacity.

When the building became available, Bob jumped on it and put his plan in place. Some walls were removed, while new walls were built, a stage was constructed, classrooms that doubled as dressing rooms on show nights took shape, and in 1972, the shop and concert series had a new home. When Bobby Kimmel discovered that, as a result of a plumbing repair, part of the restroom floor had been removed, he asked Bob Riskin what should be done. Bob suggested Bobby replace the tiles himself, which he did, cementing his legacy as McCabe's first concert director. If you use the men's restroom today, the floor tile reads "Bobby Kimmel '72."

McCabe's could now accommodate up to 150 people per show, and the increased capacity was timed well with the resurgence of interest in American roots music. This was fueled, in part, by the 1971 release of singer, songwriter and banjo player John Hartford's *Aereo-Plain* album.

McCabe's Guitar Shop storefront. *Photo by Camila Wilson.*

McCabe's Guitar Shop doorway. *Courtesy of McCabe's Guitar Shop.*

Fusing clever, contemporary songwriting to the sounds of acoustic instruments performed with great skill by fiddler Vassar Clements, guitarist Norman Blake, and Dobro player Tut Taylor (all of whom would go on to headline with their own bands and play at McCabe's), the recording helped bring bluegrass to the attention of a younger audience. Often referred to as the first "hippie bluegrass album," *Aereo-Plain* inspired a new crop of musicians who could see the possibility of channeling the energy of the rock 'n' roll they had grown up with into acoustic-based instruments. John Hartford would perform a number of solo shows at McCabe's over the years that are among the most cherished for many audience members.

Tony Trischka, who performed at McCabe's as a solo artist, with his band Skyline, and with Earl Jam, his tribute to Earl Scruggs, has been heralded as one of the most accomplished and soulful banjo players since his emergence into the world of bluegrass in the 1960s. He has recorded numerous albums exploring both the roots of the five-string and expanding its boundaries with his progressive explorations. Trischka is also a highly regarded teacher, and one of his first students was Béla Fleck, who would go on to take the banjo farther into unchartered territory (Béla played McCabe's in 1984 as a member of the New Grass Revival).

Tony explained the huge impact of the John Hartford recording: "*Aereo-Plain* blew open the barn doors for acoustic music. The songs are great, it's so much fun, and so creative, with John's way of thinking and stream of consciousness."

He also noticed a definite shift in the audiences at the bluegrass festivals he attended and performed at with his culinary-named groups, including Breakfast Special, Country Granola, and Country Cooking. Older, lawn-chaired, and younger, long-haired fans, as well as an increasing number of motorcycle gangs, coexisted as the music's appeal bridged the generation gap.

Mark O'Connor, a child prodigy who won nearly every major fiddle and flat-picking guitar contest in the United States as a young teen and who would go on to perform numerous times at McCabe's, also holds the *Aereo-Plain* album in great esteem: "It was obvious that the new grass music Hartford was inventing was going to be something I wanted to be on the front edge of as well, even as a kid. It spoke to me right from the start. I played and loved traditional music, but I liked the progressive stuff even better because I felt I could be more creative with it. And that sums up John Hartford himself. A lover and expert at traditional music but always messing around with it. I liked that approach."

As it turned out, John Hartford, Norman Blake, and Tut Taylor accompanied Mark on his 1976 album *Pickin' in the Wind* that was recorded when Mark was thirteen years old.

Even more influential was the 1972 release of *Will the Circle Be Unbroken* by the Nitty Gritty Dirt Band. Formed in 1966, the band originally featured Jeff Hannah, Jimmie Fadden, Ralph Barr, Les Thompson, Bruce Kunkel, and Jackson Browne, performing bluegrass and jug band music on a variety of acoustic instruments. The young group had spent most of their time hanging out at McCabe's Guitar Shop (the Long Beach location), and when Jackson left to pursue a solo career, he was replaced by banjo ace John McEuen.

In his autobiography, *The Life I've Picked*, John McEuen states that the Long Beach McCabe's turned out to be his gateway into the music business. He spent most of his spare time at the shop, picking with and learning tunes from other like-minded teenagers. He bought his first banjo at McCabe's, taught lessons at the shop, and eventually took the stage in the back room in Santa Monica.

Music journalist Phil Gallo recalled seeing John's first show at McCabe's. Wearing two different colored socks and playing solo, John managed to perform the inevitable instrumental "Dueling Banjos," his dueling opponent a tape recorder.

The *Circle* album, a triple LP, found the young Dirt Band re-creating country and bluegrass classics with the living legends of the trade, including Earl Scruggs, Jimmy Martin, Doc Watson, Roy Acuff, Mother Maybelle Carter, and Merle Travis. The recording is credited with simultaneously bridging both the generation and music gaps, as the coastal California Nitty Gritty hippies played side by side with their clean-cut counterparts from the rural South.

Mark O'Connor said, "The *Circle* album influenced me so much as an eleven-year-old student of old-time fiddle and bluegrass in Seattle. As a child, I would literally take the LP album cover to sleep with me at night." The circle did remain unbroken, as Mark eventually befriended John McEuen and often performed with him, including in a show at McCabe's in 1982. Then in 1984, John asked Mark to play fiddle on the Dirt Band's single "High Horse," which served as the catalyst for his record deal with Warner Brothers and created the demand for his services as a session musician, leading to 450 appearances over the next six years. Then in 1989, the Nitty Gritty Dirt Band decided to record *Will the Circle Be Unbroken II*, and this time, it was Mark O'Connor handling the fiddle position throughout the album.

The original album went on to sell more than 1 million copies.

Another factor came into play in 1973 that would greatly enhance McCabe's ability to attract audiences to Santa Monica. The Ash Grove, the legendary go-to venue for folk, blues, and bluegrass music since it opened in 1958, closed due to fire damage. This brought even more artists and audiences to McCabe's Guitar Shop.

While the folding chairs still needed to be set up on concert nights, the new venue had a permanent stage, which, legend has it, Linda Ronstadt helped paint, and a much-improved sound system.

Molly McCabe recalled being at the first concert in the new shop. It featured two bluegrass bands, Gross Junction and Elson, Lanners & Cloud, two groups led by McCabe's music instructors, John Zehnder and Pat Cloud, respectively. "There was a recording room on the second floor of the store and there was a hole in the floor, and I could lie on the floor on my stomach and watch the stage from up there, which is something I preferred," said McCabe.

Many times, this recording room was the only place where staff and family could see the concerts, as the place was packed on most show nights. Hally McCabe also watched her share of concerts from the second floor viewing spot favored by her sister. She also remembered seeing many special guests sitting on the set of stairs that were constructed on stage right that went up to the dressing rooms on the second floor.

Maple Byrne, a tour manager and instrument technician for Steve Martin, Emmylou Harris, Lyle Lovett, and Steve Goodman, among others, also preferred the hole in the floor over sitting in the tightly packed room with the rest of the audience. He vividly remembered watching Elizabeth Cotten from the perch. A guitar picker himself, he had spent his teenage years in Kansas City teaching young guitarists Cotten's signature tune "Freight Train" right-handed. He recalled, "She was one of the most charming entertainers you'd could ever see in a million years. I was just overwhelmed by that close-up view of her picking hand." Seeing the left-handed guitarist play the bass notes with three fingers and the melody with her thumb rocked his world so much he had to leave before the second show.

While he was rarely at the shop, Gerry McCabe was known to show up on concert nights. Hally recalled, "My dad loved the concerts. He would always just drop in—he never told you he was coming—it didn't matter if it was sold out. And if they had some new folks [at the door] who didn't know who he was, he would just say 'I'm McCabe,' and just walk right in."

In 1974, someone else would walk right in and have a major effect on the trajectory of the Live at McCabe's Guitar Shop concert series. Her name was Nancy Covey.

8
MOVING OUT

"My mom bought her first guitar at McCabe's," recalled Nancy Covey, who visited the shop on occasion, finding it "a friendly place to go" while she was growing up.

Nancy left Los Angeles to go to college and then "went off to Europe and disappeared for a couple of years. Then I was in Oregon, and I was going to be a teacher." In 1974, Nancy came down to visit her parents in Los Angeles and needed fifty dollars for gas to get back to Oregon, so she decided to stop in at McCabe's (a place famous for helping folks with needed travel funds).

"Does anybody need babysitting or cleaning…anything? I'll take any job," she said.

Bobby Kimmel happened to be in the store that day and took Nancy up on her offer.

"The first thing I did was clean his girlfriend's house.…And the same day, Wayne Griffith was there refinishing the floors."

When Nancy returned, Bobby asked if she could make some phone calls for him. Sure, she could do that.

The timing of Nancy's arrival was opportune—well beyond the need to tidy up Bobby's girlfriend's apartment. Just as Gerry McCabe, Walter Camp, and Bob Riskin saw the possibility of expanding the store's reach by opening branches at the Ash Grove and the Troubadour, Bobby Kimmel saw an opportunity to expand the Live at McCabe's Guitar Shop brand by presenting concerts at larger venues in the Los Angeles area and beyond. In fact, Nancy's next job was to deliver some posters for a "McCabe's Presents" concert in Santa Barbara.

"I thought she was really bright and really capable, so I started giving her more and more things to do," recalled Bobby. He offered to hire Nancy at the rate of seventy-five dollars per week for a period of six months to assist him in his role as McCabe's concert director and to work the shows outside the venue. Nancy found the work a natural fit and readily agreed. She never returned to Oregon.

With Doc and Merle Watson regularly selling out their shows at the store, Bobby Kimmel decided that presenting the popular duo in a larger venue could be a good way to start putting McCabe's on the road. So, he booked shows at the Pilgrimage Theatre in West Hollywood and a few other venues and included an opening act that was sure to seal the deal.

In March 1974, bluegrass fiddle players Vassar Clements and Richard Greene were scheduled to play a double bill at the Great American Music Hall in San Francisco for a two-night stand. Richard had invited mandolinist David Grisman to accompany him, and he, in turn, asked some other musical friends to come along for the ride, including Jerry Garcia on banjo, David Nichtern on guitar, and none other than former Rising Son Taj Mahal on upright bass, among others.

It turned out to be a very enjoyable ride, and when they decided to play a few shows touring as the Great American Music Band, Bobby Kimmel brought them in to open the Doc and Merle tour. The first show was made even more memorable when Maria Muldaur, who was riding high on the success of her top ten hit single "Midnight at the Oasis" (which was written by the band's guitarist David Nichtern), appeared as special guest vocalist with the Great American Music Band.

While the all-star band was short-lived, its repertoire, drawn from traditional fiddle tunes, swing from the Hot Club of France, bluegrass, ragtime, and jazz, spawned "Dawg music" and the creation of the revolutionary David Grisman Quintet the following year, which would go on to headline its own shows at McCabe's Guitar Shop.

While Bobby was able to put the "McCabe's Presents" stamp on the concerts held outside of the venue, the financial responsibility was all his and his co-promoters'. He offered Nancy a 15 percent share in the tour, which she readily accepted. Little did Nancy know that meant she was also liable for the same percentage if the concerts lost money—which they did.

Undeterred, Bobby sought out additional ways to put McCabe's on the road. He didn't have long to wait, and when he heard that his friends Doc and Merle Watson were touring with the New Grass Revival, McCabe's agreed to coordinate their six-city West Coast tour in October 1974.

McCabe's on the Road with the Great American Music Band. *Left to right*: David Grisman, Jerry Garcia, Maria Muldaur, Taj Mahal, and David Nichtern. *Photo by Nick Viani, www.flickr.com/photos/jnviani.*

The New Grass Revival was formed in 1971 by Kentucky-born fiddle champ and mandolin virtuoso Sam Bush. Inspired by the progressive sounds of the New Deal String Band and John Hartford's *Aereo-Plain* LP, New Grass Revival played acoustic music fueled by rock 'n' roll, and the repertoire on their debut 1972 self-titled album ranged from "Lonesome Fiddle Blues" to "Great Balls of Fire."

Sam Bush recalled the tour distinctly: "The band at that time was Courtney Johnson on banjo; Curtis Burch on Dobro and guitar; me on mandolin, fiddle, and guitar; Butch Robbins was playing electric bass with us; and we tried a drummer. His name was Michael Quinn."

Merle Watson's own four-piece band, Frosty Morn, was also on the tour, and with Nancy Covey and Bobby Kimmel traveling along, it was, according to Sam Bush, the "Rolling Watson Revue."

Sam Bush continued:

> *Through that tour was how we got to know Doc and Merle better. Doc and Merle and Rosalie* [Doc Watson's wife] *were traveling in a camper, and we would go hang with them and listen to the Allman Brothers. Doc*

McCabe's on the Road. *Pictured*: Doc and Merle Watson, Sam Bush and the New Grass Revival, Bobby Kimmel, Nancy Covey, and crew. *Courtesy of McCabe's Guitar Shop.*

> *loved 'em. That was such a happy time....I was in hog heaven. When we continued on up through Northern California, we drove through the redwoods. We got out, and there was this one gigantic redwood tree, and we all went inside the redwood tree, and Doc sang some sort of old gospel song inside the redwood. It was a goose-bump moment at the time, and it still is.*

McCabe's continued to present concerts in a number of area theaters, including shows by Little Feat, Boys of the Lough; the double bills of Bonnie Raitt and Tom Waits, Stephane Grappelli and David Grisman, and Tom Paxton and Mimi Farina; as well as the Malibu Mountains Bluegrass Carnival, which drew over ten thousand music fans.

9

MOVING ON

Back at McCabe's, Nancy Covey's six-month tenure expired, and Bobby Kimmel explained that as much as he valued her assistance, he could no longer afford to keep her on the payroll. But Nancy Covey was hooked and agreed to work without pay until the red ink turned black, and she took a job cleaning the nearby Takoma recording studio to make money. Eventually, McCabe's was able to start paying her again.

The combination of the McCabe's On the Road concerts and the regular schedule in the store's back room found the concert director and his assistant seriously multitasking. Bobby recalled that the turning point in their relationship came when he was busy on the phone and another line started ringing. "Nancy, can you get that?" And she said, "I'm on the phone, too. I'm just as busy as you are." That did it—Bobby made Nancy his partner, and they shared responsibilities equally until he left the job in 1975.

While the Live at McCabe's concerts continued to gain momentum, fueled by Bobby and Nancy's creative instincts, the series was not turning much, if any, profit. As much as the artists performing at the venue loved the place, they still demanded equal pay for equal work (what they were receiving at other venues). Without any income from sources that clubs had—the sale of alcoholic beverages—or nonprofit theaters could garner through grants and municipal funding, McCabe's relied exclusively on ticket sales to cover expenses. While most of McCabe's deals with artists consisted of a 50/50 split of ticket sales revenue, that still left very little to pay for concert staff, marketing, and other related costs.

At the end of the year, as Bobby closed the books, he was worried when he saw that the income generated by the ticket sales did not meet the direct costs of the concerts. However, when he brought his concern to Bob Riskin, he was consoled when the store owner said, "Bobby, it doesn't matter. You bring anywhere from fifty to three hundred people through that door every weekend. If one of them buys a guitar, we made money."

He felt better, but Bobby Kimmel still tried to at least get the concerts to pay for themselves. So, he staged benefit concerts that were headlined by his former bandmate Linda Ronstadt.

At the end of 1974, he booked Emmylou Harris, who had emerged on the scene as Gram Parsons's singing partner, to open some shows for the bluegrass band the Country Gazette. She returned three months later to sell out McCabe's as a headliner, hot on the heels of the release of her first solo album, *Pieces of the Sky*.

One of the concerts Bobby recalled most vividly was that of bluegrass banjo great J.D. Crowe. Bobby booked him to play two shows at McCabe's in August 1975. Little did he know that the banjoist's current band, called the New South, included guitarist Tony Rice, mandolinist/fiddler Ricky Skaggs, Bobby Sloan on bass, and nineteen-year-old Jerry Douglas on Dobro. Bobby said, "I had never heard anybody sing bluegrass like that… and I had heard a lot of bluegrass. They were so good that when they left McCabe's and went to play a show in San Francisco, I followed them up there. I wanted to hear it again."

Also in the audience that night was aspiring guitarist Larry Campbell:

> *I moved out to L.A. in 1973 to get rich and famous, starved for the first six months, and I would play for coins on the street. I ended up having a roommate who told me about McCabe's, and he took me there to see* [Texas-style fiddler] *Benny Thomasson. I was blown away by the place…that you could have a venue in a music store with all of these beautiful instruments hanging on the wall. I distinctly remember the vibe… the people who were working were just thrilled to have you there. They welcomed you like you were guests instead of a paying audience. It just felt like you were going to be part of this experience, and they were glad to have you.*

Larry went to many shows at McCabe's while living in Los Angeles: Doc and Merle Watson ("What a great venue to see those guys in."), Byron Berline, Dan Crary, as well as that J.D. Crowe and the New South concert.

"That band just blew me away. I was just totally absorbed in the traditional bluegrass thing...and to see these younger guys who were just on fire with their energy and vocabulary...an almost a rock 'n' roll attitude."

In addition to the concerts, Larry found great significance in being surrounded by the guitars hanging on the walls. "It established that you were in a house of music. That's what that place was for, and, wanting with every fiber of my being to be a successful professional musician, and hearing the music in there, seeing the instruments in there...it was a totally inspirational experience for me. I would walk out of there after every show feeling like 'Yeah, I can do this....I'm *gonna* do this."

And he did. He was soon invited to join Ben Marney's group, which served as the house band at the Palomino Club in Los Angeles. The band had relocated to Mississippi when Ben Marney bought a nightclub there, and then Larry decided to "get some anxiety back" into his life and went back to New York. But he would return to finally get an opportunity to play at McCabe's.

Bobby Kimmel also had rambling on his mind and felt as though he had given McCabe's all that he could, and he was ready to resume his own music career (and in fact went on to tour playing bass with Doc and Merle Watson). He called Nancy Covey: "Come get the keys. I'm not coming in." When Nancy asked who was now going to run the concert series, he answered, "You are."

10

SINGERS AND SONGWRITERS

Soon after passing his keys on to Nancy, Bobby Kimmel checked in to see if she needed anything. Nancy replied, "Nope—I got this."

This would turn out to be a major understatement, as Nancy quickly went about expanding the reach and programming at McCabe's—although attracting artists to play there could be a challenge.

Nancy said, "McCabe's was not trendy. We were on the west side of L.A. In those days, Santa Monica was not the place to be—it was totally not cool—grannies live out here. I never could understand that, because I thought, 'We have the beach.' So, I had to work hard to get the people I got. I was ambitious. I was just driven to do a really good job."

Nancy started suggesting to some of the artists who lived locally and fronted full groups that they should leave their bandmates behind for the weekend for a chance to play solo in the intimacy of McCabe's. "This was before the term *unplugged* came. I remember pitching people on the concept."

Nancy soon realized she could combine her passions for both music and travel by taking excursions to festivals to discover new artists to play the venue. A friend who was a travel agent gave Nancy the idea to bring other music fans with her on her planned trek to the Vancouver Folk Festival. Nancy could encourage audiences at McCabe's to take the trip, and her friend would take care of the details and act as the group's leader. However, when not enough people signed up, the travel agent told Nancy that he couldn't afford to come along. When she asked, "Well, who is going to lead the tour?" Nancy received a response she was getting used to hearing: "You are."

And of course she did, and when the travel agent suggested they work together on the next trip to the New Orleans Jazz Festival, Nancy demurred, realizing she could take care of all the details herself. And of course she did, which, in turn, ignited the creation of Festival Tours, a business that Nancy would lead from that day forward.

On a trip to England to attend the Cambridge Folk Festival, Nancy met American singer and songwriter Loudon Wainwright III through their mutual friends in the Boys of the Lough, a Celtic band that was playing there.

Loudon emerged in the early 1970s with songs that were well steeped in cynical humor, candid personal observations, and social commentary. While his critically acclaimed confessional songcraft started to develop a cult following, it was his novelty song "Dead Skunk in the Middle of the Road" and his appearance as an actor in the television show *M*A*S*H* that elevated his career. When on tour in Los Angeles, he would typically play the Troubadour. However, Nancy asked him to consider playing McCabe's his next time through the city.

Sure enough, Loudon was booked to play McCabe's in 1978 and arrived to find out two things: (1) Takoma Records had a studio two doors down from McCabe's and could connect a cable to the venue, so he could record his concert with the possibility of including tracks on his planned live album, and (2) McCabe's did not serve alcohol, creating an environment he was not accustomed to playing in.

Just as Nancy had convinced Loudon that he should play at McCabe's, Loudon used his own charisma to persuade Nancy to offer complimentary champagne to the audience to loosen things up a bit. In an interview in 2024, Loudon did not specifically recall the incident but was quick to add, "Sounds like a thing I might have done at that time."

It did happen, and it was the first time McCabe's ever bent its rules about not serving alcohol. Nancy recalled filling up paper cups with champagne for the audience members. Songs from the concert, along with selections from English concert halls in Birmingham and Manchester, appear on Loudon's 1979 release, *A Live One*.

Loudon recalled, "Once I played the club for the first time, I really loved it….The ambiance with all the guitars on the walls. All the legends of acoustic music played that room…my first big musical heroes Ramblin' Jack Elliott and Dave Van Ronk."

In fact, Loudon has returned time and time again—without champagne. When asked why he thought McCabe's survived the test of time, he responded in typical fashion, "It has stayed the same in a good kind of way. Good vibe, good sound system....Maybe because it was not a bar."

Mary Katherine Aldin, who was immersed in the Los Angeles music scene, working at the Ash Grove, Folklore Productions, and a local record store while hosting a number of radio shows, recalled that McCabe's no-booze environment was a plus for one of Loudon's heroes, Greenwich Village folk and blues stalwart Dave Van Ronk. "He had played at the Ash Grove many times, and we became really good friends. When he came out to play at McCabe's, he had stopped drinking, and he was absolutely terrific. He was funny, and he was smart. Everybody loved him. Dave loved McCabe's," she said.

After one of his concerts, Mary Katherine accompanied Dave back to his hotel to catch up on old times. "We went across the street to the room and sat around and talked for a while, and then he said, 'I'm glad I don't drink, or I would go across the street to McCabe's and get a drink.' And I said, 'No you wouldn't. They don't have anything to drink except weak coffee.' And he laughed and said, 'Then it's good thing that I don't drink anymore.'"

While Nancy was ever resourceful in seeking and finding new talent, on occasion, some discoveries were delivered to her doorstep. When Nancy was negotiating with John Lee Hooker's booking agent to secure a date with the musician responsible for the classic songs "Boogie Chillen" and "Boom Boom," the deal came with the requirement that the show be opened by a then relatively unknown singer/songwriter, John Hiatt. Although Nancy had never heard of John Hiatt and typically preferred to choose her own supporting acts, she agreed to the terms in order to present the blues legend at McCabe's.

Born and raised in Indianapolis, Indiana, John Hiatt wrote his first song at the age of eleven and learned to play guitar and performed in some teenage bands before he quit school and moved to Nashville. Hired as a songwriter by Tree Publishing Music International, John released a couple of albums on Epic Records, which did not meet sales expectations (although one of his songs, "Sure as I'm Sittin' Here," was covered by Three Dog Night and made it into the top twenty in 1974). Once he was dropped from Epic, John recalled that Mike Kappus, the owner of the Rosebud Agency who was now booking his concert tours, thought a change of scene might do him some good. "Come on out to San Francisco, and I can book you from out here." John stayed only a year. "The clouds rolled in every day at 3 p.m....It was depressing," he said.

Nancy recalled her reaction to hearing John Hiatt for the first time: "Oh my God! This guy is great! So, I immediately booked him again and kept booking him." As it turned out, John relocated to Los Angeles, which made it even easier for him to build his audience at McCabe's, and he opened shows for Mike Bloomfield and David Bromberg. McCabe's would prove to play a pivotal part in his career a few years later.

Throughout her tenure as concert director, Nancy found ways to bring both emerging and established artists to the stage in the back room of McCabe's Guitar Shop.

In the late '60s, Joseph Henry "T Bone" Burnett moved to Los Angeles from Fort Worth, Texas, where he had been a member of a folk rock band and opened up his own recording studio after graduating high school. He said, "The first show I went to there was to see Oscar Peterson with Ray Brown in the Cocoanut Grove at the Ambassador Hotel, where Robert Kennedy was assassinated. The second place I went was to McCabe's—one of the singers was Linda Carey, who later married Rodney Dillard, and the drummer was Jim Keltner, who became a lifelong friend." The band was MC Squared, who had released a few singles but whose full-length album was shelved until it was released in 2012.

After recording his own 1972 debut, T Bone toured with Delaney & Bonnie and, in 1975, joined Bob Dylan's Rolling Thunder Revue tour, which, in turn, spawned the Alpha Band—T Bone, Steven Soles, and David Mansfield—a group that released three albums. In the early '80s, T Bone resumed his solo career, and Nancy Covey booked him on a regular basis, pairing him with artists such as Ranchers for Peace, the Del Fuegos, and Guy Clark.

When Elvis Costello, who had become an international pop star in the late 1970s with his band the Attractions, embarked on a solo tour, T Bone was the opening act, and the two became great friends and recorded some tracks together as the Coward Brothers. When he was home, T Bone continued to attend concerts at McCabe's. He said:

> *I've seen some of the best shows I've ever seen there, foremost among them was sitting on the stairs with Elvis Costello to see Bill Monroe. Before the show, Elvis and I were hanging out in the dressing room when Monroe came in rubbing his eyes, having just woken up on the bus outside and walked in, put on his hat, climbed down to the stage and played a transcendent set. I don't remember who was in the Bluegrass Boys at that time, but Bill Monroe was seriously great. It was one of the handful of best shows I've ever seen anywhere, and Elvis says the same thing.*

T Bone would later put together a series of "Christmas at McCabe's' shows in 1991 for National Public Radio, with Harry Shearer, Sam Phillips, Leo Kottke, Michael Penn, Van Dyke Parks, Stan Freberg, Bob Neuwirth, Jeff Bridges, Victoria Williams, Joe Henry, Mark O'Connor, Edgar Meyer, Jerry Douglas, and Booker T. Jones.

While T Bone continued to record his own music, his career as one of the most in-demand producers of Americana music and movie soundtracks was skyrocketing. In fact, his work on the Coen brothers' films *O Brother, Where Art Thou?* and *Inside Llewyn Davis* would be chiefly responsible for a resurgence in the interest in bluegrass and folk music, respectively, in the early 2000s, building new audiences for American roots music across the country, including at McCabe's Guitar Shop. T Bone's eventual move to Nashville made his visits to McCabe's less frequent. However, in 2024, he released the Grammy-nominated album *The Other Side*, and when he embarked on his first tour in over two decades in 2025, he chose to play a three-night, six-concert stand at McCabe's Guitar Shop. All six shows sold out as music fans, including Ringo Starr (T Bone produced Ringo's 2025 album *Look Up*), welcomed T Bone back to McCabe's.

Growing up in Southern California, Rosanne Cash, the eldest daughter of country music icon Johnny Cash, went to many concerts—but not at McCabe's Guitar Shop. "No, I didn't know about McCabe's when I was a kid," she said. "I was in my very early twenties when I learned about it. I saw Peter, Paul and Mary at an outdoor concert in Santa Barbara and saw Donovan separately at the same venue and the Steve Miller Band at the Ventura Theater. I saw Emmylou, of course, and George Benson at Universal Amphitheater. I remember I wore a long black dress with sparkles on it to see the Stones. My dad got tickets for me and three of my friends. It was thrilling."

After high school, Rosanne spent some time touring with her dad. In 1978, she teamed up with singer/songwriter Rodney Crowell to record her first album and started touring with his band the Cherry Bombs. One of her early shows was held at McCabe's. "I was very intimidated and nervous… pretty unformed and shy. I couldn't keep up with Albert Lee [the band's guitarist], and I'm sure there was a lot of eye-rolling at my attempts."

Soon after, Rosanne started recording for Columbia and topped the country music charts with the songs "Seven Year Ache," "My Baby Thinks He's a Train," and "Blue Moon with Heartache."

Rosanne hit number one with four songs from her 1987 album, *King's Record Shop*, and she was named Billboard's Top Singles Artist in 1988. Rosanne made a special guest appearance at McCabe's that same year in a concert by Rodney Crowell and fiddler Stuart Duncan. "I got up and sang a couple of songs," she said. "Again, intimidated. McCabe's had a serious reputation among musicians for its highly refined and curated list of performers, and I was comparing myself to all of them."

Rosanne returned in 1990 to headline a show accompanied by guitarist Steuart Smith and bassist Jim Hanson. Her mother Vivian was in the audience that night. "My mom came to a few shows—the Greek Theater, a show in Reno, a couple more—but it was really fun that she came that night. I remember Steuart—who was also aware of the giants who had played there and felt the pressure to add up—came off stage at the end of the show really depressed and criticizing himself. He was really dark for the rest of the night. He felt he didn't play his best and spent hours castigating himself. He had played phenomenally, of course."

When, in 1996, Rosanne released her first album on Capitol Records, *10 Song Demo*, a relatively stripped-down collection of compositions that lent themselves to being performed live in intimate performance venues, she returned to McCabe's for two sold-out concerts that would prove to be particularly memorable for her accompanist. Larry Campbell, who had attended concerts at McCabe's many years before as a young musician and had aspired to play the historic room one day himself, provided his formidable skills on guitar and mandolin that night. "That was a really big deal to me," he said. "To be performing in that place it felt like a dream come true."

The following year, Larry joined Bob Dylan's Never Ending Tour band for eight years and was subsequently the music director of Levon Helm's Midnight Ramble Band.

In 2015, Larry returned to McCabe's to perform a show with Jorma Kaukonen, and that same year, Jackson Browne asked if Larry could join him on a tour to substitute for his regular guitarist Val McCallum, who was unable to participate. He readily agreed, and he and his musical partner Teresa Williams opened the shows on the tour, backed by Jackson's band.

Then, when Larry and Teresa were booked to headline a concert at McCabe's in 2018, Jackson attended and sat in with them, "That was a wonderful night," Larry said. "There's another full circle moment, because Jackson Browne was L.A. to me. When I was out there struggling—he was a hometown hero there—and to play this place and have him on stage with us…what a great feeling that was."

While playing the McCabe's stage was one of Larry's musical goals, he was not particularly intimidated by the experience. "It's such a comfortable, easy place to perform. You just feel relaxed...like you're in someone's living room and having an experience with a bunch of people."

Reflecting on her experiences playing live at McCabe's Guitar Shop, Rosanne said, "It was so *important*. It was a cultural touchstone. The standard of excellence has never diminished. It's an honor to be asked to perform there. The authenticity of purpose and the connection to the community of musicians is what gives it the staying power. McCabe's loves real musicians, and we love it back."

11
SOME ENCHANTING EVENINGS

The ever-increasing quality and diversity of shows at McCabe's continued to expand the audience and attract music aficionados who spent quite a bit of time hanging out at the store and going to concerts—among them, John Chelew.

A California native whose love for folk music was piqued as a young teenager in 1964, when he saw Peter, Paul and Mary at the Monterey Folk Festival, John moved to west Los Angeles in the 1970s, and there, he worked at the Regent Theatre. He started attending numerous concerts at McCabe's and soon struck up a friendship with Nancy Covey. Before long, he was hired as her assistant.

Nancy recalled, "John would just come out and hang out at the shows. John was a good source of interesting things and was very tuned in to the English scene." One of the musicians John encouraged Nancy to book was Richard Thompson, an artist who was unfamiliar to Nancy at the time.

Having cofounded the groundbreaking group Fairport Convention as a teenager in the '60s, Richard Thompson and his bandmates are credited with developing a very distinctive style of British folk rock. Richard left the group at the age of twenty-one to create a decade-long musical partnership with his then-wife, Linda. Richard was just launching his solo career when Nancy contacted his manager, Jo Lustig, to see about the possibility of booking a McCabe's show. However, the offer was turned down, as Jo was hoping to present Richard's solo debut in the United States in a larger venue with a higher performance fee.

While British folk rock enthusiasts were certainly aware of Richard Thompson, Nancy did not believe he had enough name recognition in the United States at that point to justify a high fee in a large venue, so no deal was made.

On one of Nancy's subsequent trips to England to satisfy her wanderlust and to look for artists to play McCabe's, she attended the Fairport Convention Festival, an annual event started in 1976 that often included a reunion of its original members as well other British folk rockers. It was there that Nancy met Richard and offered to present him at McCabe's; she also offered to line up some other gigs for him on the California coast. Richard agreed, and Nancy went about securing dates in other venues and booking interviews to publicize the concerts on various radio shows.

The tour commenced at McCabe's, and Richard Thompson recalled walking into the venue for the very first time:

> *It felt very folksy and very hippie 1960s in a not unpleasant way. I had not played in the U.S. since touring with Fairport, Iain Matthews, and Sandy Denny—probably the last of those was 1971. The very first show I did, I was thoroughly jet lagged. Set one was a struggle, but I got through it. Set two, which started at about 5 a.m. UK time, was a miracle. I didn't know you could actually play in your sleep, but I did. Of course, that was the show that people loved and reacted to the most positively, but I dreamt it all.*

Mary Katherine Aldin, who was working for Folklore Productions at the time, attended Richard's McCabe's debut with the booking agency's founder, Manny Greenhill. She had seen Richard with Fairport Convention years before at the Troubadour and subsequently became a fan of his work with Linda Thompson. She was a little taken aback when Richard took the stage solo. "I thought I was going to hear Richard and Linda Thompson," she said. "When I heard his songwriting, I was really knocked out and duly impressed with his talent."

Steve Hochman, who, several years later, would become a music writer for the *Los Angeles Times*, had his McCabe's initiation along with Richard Thompson that night: "I had become something of a Fairport Convention fan in the '70s and then discovered Richard and Linda Thompson's catalog, becoming completely immersed in Richard's songs and guitar playing. The release of *Shoot Out the Lights* [Richard and Linda's final album together] really hit me hard."

When Steve heard that Richard was stateside and playing McCabe's, he arrived early, before the doors opened, and was first in line. He managed to grab front-row seats. "I was completely transfixed," he said. "The store, the guitars lining the walls, and seeing this person whose music had completely entranced me perform. Just seeing him alone—the guitar playing, the tone of the songs, his quips in between songs—not only that, I fell for the experience at McCabe's."

Apparently, Richard's struggle to remain awake during his show was not evident to the audience, and afterward, he managed to participate in a lengthy interview about the definition of folk music with Robert Lloyd, a journalist with *LA Weekly* at the time who was also a musician and would become a frequent presence on McCabe's stage.

There was little doubt that Richard was not particularly concerned with working within the constraints of any particular musical genre. His songs, guitar playing, and vocal delivery were like none other, and his American solo debut at McCabe's proved to be the spark that brought him great admiration in the States. The *Los Angeles Times* went on to call him the finest rock songwriter after Dylan and the best electric guitarist since Hendrix and *Rolling Stone* named him one of the "Top 100 Guitarists of All Time." His song "1952 Vincent Black Lightning" was named one of *TIME* magazine's "100 Greatest Songs Since 1923."

At the time, Nancy was just delighted that the shows sold really well, and she presented Richard with a bonus: a new guitar case from McCabe's.

As Richard and Nancy spent more time together, it wasn't long before a romance blossomed, and the couple began splitting their time between California and England. They were eventually married in 1985, and years later, their son Jack worked and performed at McCabe's.

Of course, McCabe's legacy as a place for more than music all started the day Bob Riskin sold Esperanza Santa Cruz that guitar back in 1966. They later got married and had two children, Nora and Jolie.

Steve Hochman, who returned to McCabe's countless times after the Richard Thompson debut, recalled two standout events that went beyond his love of music. Steve was somewhat acquainted with writer Mary Herczog, but when they both attended a concert by Steve Wynn and John Wesley Harding in 1990, they ended up chatting, having dinner, and dating—and eventually, they got married. Mary passed away in 2010, but then in 2018, Steve was once again at McCabe's, this time to see a show by Bob Neuwirth. There, he first connected with playwright, writer, and poet Susan Hayden under the imaginary McCabe's mistletoe, and they, too, were eventually married. Susan's son Mason Summit worked at the store and performs as part of the duo the Prickly Pair, who have played the stage at McCabe's.

When New Yorker Gary Calamar landed in Los Angeles, he proceeded to become a record store manager, a public radio host, and a music supervisor for movies and television, and he had a stint as manager of the band the Balancing Act. Gary spent a fair amount of time attending shows at McCabe's and vividly recalled one enchanting evening: "It was May 18, 1990. Dave Alvin was playing along with Syd Straw, and it was between sets. Mingling amidst the metronomes and the jaw harps, I was about to grab a few more free guitar picks when I saw her, Alice. She was with our mutual friend Nancy Sefton, who went on to become Dave's manager. *Zing* went the strings of my heart. There was a hum in the room, and everything was in perfect tune. Eighteen years later, we came into the store to buy Zoe, our then-six-year-old daughter, her first guitar!"

Longtime music teacher Fred Sokolow met his wife, Lynn, at a group lesson, and their son Zach worked at the store and has taken the stage with his band the Americans.

Romance aside, McCabe's, on occasion, has also become a catalyst for some business ventures. Sandy Goldfarb, who had done some publicity work in New York before moving west, went to see singer/songwriter Bob Gibson, whom she had encountered in 1965 during a folk festival at Carnegie Hall. Sandy recalled that once they became reacquainted and Bob heard of her PR credentials, he said, "You should be a publicist, and I should be your first client." "So," she said, "Sandy Goldfarb Public Relations was born in McCabe's."

Jeanine Frank was a huge fan of jazz pianist Dave Frishberg, and when she heard he was appearing at McCabe's, she went. The two became friends, and once she started presenting "Parlor Performances" in living rooms all over town, Dave became a regular. Over the next twenty years, Jeanine went on to produce dozens of his shows.

But for most, it was not the birth of a business venture or a honeymoon that made for a memorable evening at McCabe's—it was the music. While regular concerts by singer/songwriter Eric Andersen were always special, his appearance in 1982 was a particular highlight. Eric, who had made his entry into the 1960s Greenwich Village scene with his anthem "Thirsty Boots," became a regular on the national folk circuit—including appearances at McCabe's—and released many acclaimed albums. Longtime Los Angeles resident Joni Mitchell, who trusted her guitar repairs to the McCabe's staff and who attended concerts there by Tom Rush and Jackson Browne, among others, was known to be a good friend of Eric's, and she credited him with turning her on to some of the open guitar tunings for which she became famous. Joni was in the audience for Eric's 1982 concert and was invited to perform as his special guest. Nearly a decade later, Joni returned to McCabe's when Eric played the room in 1991, singing harmony on his song "Blue River," which they had recorded together. Then she was granted the stage to perform two songs herself: "Cherokee Louise" and "How Do You Stop."

Over twenty-five years would go by before Joni again was at McCabe's to see Eric, but this time, she simply enjoyed the concert in her seat in the front row. A couple years earlier, she had suffered a brain aneurysm that left her unable to sing, talk, play guitar, or walk; however, the fact that Eric and his band were in town ultimately became a major factor in Joni's recovery and return to performing. In a post on Joni Mitchell's Facebook fan page, Eric recounts that when she was recuperating in 2017, she came to see his show at McCabe's, and then the band went up to her house to play for her up close for one of several special evenings over the next two years. He remembered putting her guitar in her lap; she held it, and although she wasn't quite ready for singing and playing yet, she hummed along on "Blue River." At the time, Eric had no idea what he had started and where it

Steve Goodman. *Photo by David Gans, www.perfectible.net.*

would lead, as these informal musical gatherings morphed and apparently turned into jams. Eventually, Joni started picking up the guitar and singing and went into full-swing rehearsals led by singer/songwriter Brandi Carlile, who brought the "Joni jams" concept to the stage at the 2022 Newport Folk Festival for Joni's historic return to public performances.

Seeing famous faces in the audience is not uncommon at McCabe's Guitar Shop. Singer/songwriter Steve Goodman, best known for his song "City of New Orleans," typically toured with a full band in large-capacity clubs and theaters, but in 1983, he was living in Seal Beach, about an hour south of Santa Monica. He decided to play a pair of solo concerts at McCabe's. Steve's tour manager Maple Byrne recalled, "He loved to get in a small room like that. He could drive himself from home. Goodman was the most intense solo performer—of any genre—that I could ever imagine. That's one of the reasons that the McCabe's dates stand out." Maple recounted that the place was packed and counted among the audience Jerry Brown, then-governor of California, and his date, Linda Ronstadt.

12
THE YEE HAW FACTOR

Steve Goodman himself was in the audience for a concert the following year, 1984, when a double bill featuring the contemporary bluegrass band Hot Rize and New Grass Revival was scheduled. It turned out be an emotional night for New Grass founder Sam Bush.

Sam met Steve Goodman in 1970, when they shared a bill at a club called the Red Dog in Louisville, Kentucky. Consequently, they struck up a friendship and kept in touch over the years. Steve had been fighting leukemia since 1969, so when Sam was diagnosed with cancer in 1982, "one of the people who encouraged me and gave me advice and what to expect… was Steve Goodman. He'd say, 'Sammy, you gotta take that chemo man.… Chemo ain't cute, but you gotta do it. Them doctors are the worst drug dealers in the world.…They don't take the stuff, they just sell it to ya.'" The last time Sam saw Steve was at that concert at McCabe's—he passed away five months later at the age of thirty-six.

Sam Bush and New Grass Revival would return to McCabe's to play shows with Mike Auldridge, Tony Rice, and Norman Blake. "Whenever you would be at McCabe's with a guitar-style show, it would be a packed house, because everyone wanted to see those guitar players. It felt like we were really doing well to get on those shows. The musicians loved to come to McCabe's, because you get to sit around in the afternoon, look at these great instruments—there would always be something we'd want to buy but never could."

Whenever New Grass Revival pulled up to a venue, they would typically assess it with a "Yee Haw Factor," a rating that would gauge the probability of the audience yelling out "Yee haw!" during their set, even though the band, while performing on instruments typically associated with bluegrass and country music, were playing music closer to rock, soul, and reggae.

When asked what level of the Yee Haw Factor McCabe's was rated, Sam stated, "McCabe's was a hip place…a classy place where there was *no* Yee Haw Factor.…People would come to hear the flat-picking of Doc [Watson] or Norman [Blake]—and where bluegrass bands were accepted as well.… All forms of picking were respected equally at McCabe's."

Peter Rowan has played McCabe's on numerous occasions, including a solo show where he was joined on stage by Gillian Welch and David Rawlings, and he concurs: "McCabe's has always been a great and supportive gig. I've played there with my brothers. Once, David Grisman and I opened for Bill Monroe. Bill offered to manage us, but we were working on *Old and in the Way* with Jerry Garcia, John Kahn, and Vassar Clements. [*Old and in the Way* was yet another influential album that helped bring audiences who were listening to bands like the Grateful Dead to bluegrass.] It would have been interesting to have Bill Monroe as our manager!"

In addition to continuing the work of presenting the most recognizable names in bluegrass, Nancy Covey made sure that the McCabe's stage was a showcase for emerging musicians as well.

Jack MacKenzie, a retail manager, repair technician, and guitarist himself, recalled one Saturday morning when a young guy came into the shop. "He picked up a mandolin and was 'noodling' around on it. I could hear that he was a competent player and asked him if he'd care to pick a tune or two. He accepted, and I grabbed a guitar. I remember asking him if he sang at all, and he said, he did. So, he sang something, and all heads in the shop turned to look at who had that beautiful, clear tenor voice. It was Vince Gill."

Vince would soon find himself on the stage in the back room of the shop. Mark O'Connor recalled:

> *It was exciting that McCabe's wanted a solo set from me as an opener when I was sixteen in 1978. I was recording my new* Markology *guitar album at the time in Berkeley with Tony Rice, David Grisman, Sam Bush, Dan Crary, and others. I was already playing solo gigs around Seattle and had a couple of local guitarists I'd use, both of them about twice as old as I was. When we realized how much it'd cost to get one of the accompanists down there to Santa Monica to play the set, it dawned on my mother and I that our young friend Vince Gill had just moved there to join Byron Berline and Dan Crary's band Sundance and that maybe he'd play the set with me. I*

stayed with him and his new girlfriend Janice Oliver (she had just formed the Sweethearts of the Rodeo duo with her sister Kristine). I was already good friends with Vince. We first met and played when he himself was sixteen and I was twelve. It was at Byron Berline's bluegrass festival in Oklahoma. We ran into each other a lot after that at the summer festivals.

My show at McCabe's was great fun, I remember. I played fiddle and guitar material. I was without a good mandolin during those years, so I commonly left it out of my shows. But anytime I could borrow one, I'd play it. I likely borrowed one at McCabe's for the show, as they had plenty hanging right there on the wall for sale. Good F-style mandolins back then were always more expensive than I could ever swing for as a teen musician. Vince sang a couple of songs, but it was mainly the instrumentals I had prepared with him while he played rhythm guitar and took some leads—Texas-style fiddle tunes, swing and blues, bluegrass, and guitar instrumentals, including some originals. I am sure I did my first guitar tune I wrote, "Pickin' in the Wind." It was cool to see all of the guitars (and mandolins) on the walls at McCabe's, but honestly, Santa Monica, California, was also one of the skateboard capitals of the world in 1978, and Vince driving me around to various skateboard parks during my visit was also pretty cool to a sixteen-year-old boarder.

Mark returned for a show in 1979:

Byron Berline was one of my mentors on the fiddle, and Dan Crary was one of my mentors on the guitar. They'd always have me sit in for a tune or two with their group whenever I was around. The show they had me do with them at McCabe's also featured Vince Gill as a new group member of Sundance. Every time I sat in, we'd play Byron's "Gold Rush" for twin fiddles. We could easily match our sound together well, and Byron got just a big kick out of that. Then we'd plow into some "Sally Goodin" and have a field day on the great war horse fiddle tune that Byron was a master with.

I remember that jazz guitarist Alan Wald was also in the Sundance group, and I had been really getting into electric jazz-rock fusion by that time. I had a '61 Les Paul and had my own electric guitar trio with bass and drums in high school back in Seattle. It was a coming-of-age time for me musically, tying all of these threads together during that particular visit at McCabe's. I was playing bluegrass, country, swing, and fiddle tunes, and there was Vince totally getting into electric guitar. And once Alan knew I was heading into jazz-rock fusion, he was encouraging me and pushing

Left to right: Byron Berline, Mark O'Connor, Vince Gill. *Photo by Marty O'Connor, from* A Musical Childhood in Pictures, *courtesy of Mark O'Connor.*

In between his concerts at McCabe's, Mark O'Connor went into the studio to record his album *On the Rampage*. That's Mark in the center in his McCabe's Guitar Shop T-shirt along with (*left to right*) Sam Bush, Bill Amatneek, David Grisman, and Tony Rice. They all played separately at McCabe's on numerous occasions. *Photo by Marty O'Connor, from* A Musical Childhood in Pictures, *courtesy of Mark O'Connor.*

> *me. That was the visit where Vince, Alan, and I were trying out a lot of electric guitars hanging on the walls at McCabe's. I was an acoustic musician still and would always be first and foremost, but* [I was] *really getting into electric that year as well.*

Two years later Mark was invited to become a permanent member of the jazz-rock fusion group the Dregs.

But before that, Mark's acoustic mastery was called on by another band:

> *In 1979, I joined the San Francisco–based acoustic ensemble David Grisman Quintet. I replaced Tony Rice as guitarist on the Martin D-28 Herringbone, while doubling on violin and mandolin (using David's extra mandolin). David Grisman was finicky about booking enough gigs for the band members to stay financially afloat. I assume there were not many venues that both wanted our kind of progressive string acoustic music and that could meet his fee requirements. So, my two bandmates, Darol Anger and Mike Marshall,* [and I] *formed a part-time trio and booked gigs for ourselves up and down the coast. And one of those shows took place at McCabe's in 1980. It was a pretty cool trio, passing back and forth the same three instruments we all played: violin, guitar, and mandolin. We did a lot of new acoustic experimental music that was a bit more "out there" than the music we were playing with Grisman at the time. If we got a good response from McCabe's audience, they were very kind to us.*

Mark returned in 1982 for the aforementioned concert with John McEuen and then came back in 1991:

> *I was ready to leave the studio career behind that I had worked so hard to attain, but I wanted an outlet to display the musical development that had been piling up inside me for years and needed to come out. It was John Hartford who convinced me that I could perform an unaccompanied solo concert on my three instruments* [fiddle, guitar, and mandolin] *like he did* [on his three instruments, fiddle, guitar, and banjo] *and leave the studio career to become a solo artist.*
>
> *I devised a solo unaccompanied instrumental show I could tour. I had pickups on each of the three acoustic instruments—violin, guitar, and mandolin—and I had the very first miniature lavalier microphone arms attached to the instruments. They were custom made for me. For this show, I was able to book clubs and small listening rooms like McCabe's.*

13
PERFECTLY GOOD GUITAR

Growing up in Santa Monica, John Zehnder was a regular customer at McCabe's. He would spend time at the store playing music and drinking coffee, and he became well known to both Walter Camp and Bob Riskin. While attending Santa Monica College and then UCLA, John worked summers in the oilfields, and in 1962, with the cash from his work burning a hole in his pocket, he walked into McCabe's and was smitten by a Martin D-28. But he hesitated to turn over the amount he needed to buy the instrument. He asked his girlfriend Elizabeth, who would soon become his wife, if she thought he should put the money into his savings account or buy the guitar. Without missing a beat, she said, "Buy the guitar!" He took her advice, and Bob Riskin converted the right-handed instrument to suit lefty John Zehnder.

Soon after, John and Elizabeth got married and moved to New Jersey, where John earned his master's degree in religious education from Princeton Theological Seminary and took a series of odd jobs to support his family, which grew to include his daughter, Laura, and twin sons, Tom and Tim.

Once McCabe's Guitar Shop opened and started selling instruments, it didn't take long to see that offering music lessons would be the next logical step. So, in 1970, when Walter Camp and Bob Riskin began looking for a trusted soul to manage the store and music school, they called John Zehnder to see if he would consider returning to Santa Monica to take the position. John turned to his wife to see if she thought he should take the job. She, again, without hesitation, told him, "Go for it!"

Bob Riskin recalled that John and his family made the entire cross-country trip with a brake line that was clamped together with a pair of vice grips. "John loved clamps," Bob said. In fact, once John arrived, he started fixing guitars and utilized his beloved clamps in countless guitar repairs. His son Tim reflected: "He was just known to tinker and figure things out for himself. He pioneered ways of using dental drills and other things that weren't being used to effect repairs....One guitar came to him in a paper bag. The forlorn owner, with tears in his eyes, had backed his camper over it." The guitar's owner told John that if he could fix it, he could keep it. John accepted the paper bag of Martin guitar pieces and, in his spare time, eventually restored the instrument.

However, John's most famous repair was not on a guitar; it was instead on an instrument that McCabe's typically did not service. Bob Riskin recalled, "Somebody brought their clarinet to the store. John looked at the clarinet, took it apart and removed the rolls of hundred-dollar bills someone had stuffed in the instrument. He put it back together and said, 'It will probably play better now.'"

John also enjoyed putting parts together to create new instruments, including a stand-up bass banjo, a ten-string banjo, and the twelve-string guitar/banjo he called the "banjar."

In addition to his skills on ukulele, banjo, mandolin, and guitar, which he taught at McCabe's, John was a great lover of wind instruments, particularly the sousaphone. Soon after arriving on the job, John distributed his collection of wind instruments to the string teachers. "Give 'em a horn—see what they can do," he said.

John Zehnder in his Blass Band getup. *Photo provided by the Zehnder family.*

Thus started a new tradition at McCabe's: a biannual performance by the "Blass Band," string pickers turned horn players who performed at a concert in a nearby park in the summer and at the holiday show at the store in December. John would lead the band while playing the sousaphone and wearing a Viking helmet. He had also somehow procured the Santa Monica High School band uniforms from the 1940s, which he put into a grab bag. He invited each member of the band to choose one uniform and wear it for the performance, provided that it did not fit properly.

Horns aside, McCabe's was known as a place that fixed guitars, and in the early 1970s, Jack MacKenzie and Larry Brown were added to the team. Jack recalled the learning curve: "Basically, I just tried things. With an unending source of 'guinea pigs' in the form of warranty repair instruments, which we were obligated to repair or replace, it made sense to try to fix them in house. So, as time wore on, I learned what not to do by doing it. It was sacrificial to a degree. But the process of discovery was a powerful and effective teacher. And as a result of this type of learning, I developed a feel for the formidable forces that assault the geometry of steel string guitars." He recalled rebuilding guitars that were brought to him in splinters, as well as repairing Steve Martin's Gibson Florentine banjo: "The binding was held on by band aids. We learned from each other. Larry Brown was confident and skilled, and brought a lot of knowledge to the circle."

Then Koichilo "Koich" Oshio, an apprenticed craftsman in traditional Japanese woodworking, was added to the team. "We established a reputation of competent repair....Folks from all over the west brought their guitars to us," Jack remembered.

One of those folks was Joni Mitchell, and one of those repairs came with a side benefit. Kit Alderson recalled, "Koichilo told me that one day, after he had worked on her guitars, that she gave him a forty-five-minute private concert in Room 1 [the green room] at McCabe's."

14
McCABE'S BECOMES ECLECTIC

Once Nancy Covey and Richard Thompson got together, she took full advantage of his broad interest in music: "He would give me a wish list—he got to sit in with a lot of people."

Richard recalled, "She would ask me if there was any artist I would like her to book. Well, in those days, living in Los Angeles, you had amazing figures from the world of jazz, blues, and folk, many retired and many long past their career high point. So, I asked for a double bill of George Van Eps—great seminal jazz guitarist who had been recording since the '30s—and country-jazz guitarist Thumbs Carllile, who played in Dobro tuning with the guitar flat on his lap."

Nancy continued to expand the musical diversity at McCabe's, keeping the blues alive with performances by Willie Dixon, Big Mama Thornton, Sippie Wallace, Clarence "Gatemouth" Brown, Johnny Shines, Robert Lockwood Jr., Dr. John, Sippie Wallace, John Hammond (once joined by George Thorogood), and Roosevelt Sykes. The venue also hosted solo concerts by Taj Mahal.

Taj recalled his return: "It was really great—first of all, these places are not known for hanging around for any length of time. McCabe's was still there and had gone on to become a valuable venue for touring artists. It was nice to see something that was still around from when I first came out to California."

Mitch Greenhill of Folklore Productions recalled Taj Mahal's enthusiasm for playing the room: "I remember that he ended his set by chanting, 'Support McCabe's!'"

Traditional Celtic artists DeDanaan, Alistair Anderson, Kevin Burke, Robin Williamson, Mick Moloney, and Eugene O'Donnell; Cajun accordionists Clifton Chenier, Jo-El Sonnier, and Rosie Ledet; the South American band Sukay; and Eastern European group Klezorim helped diversify McCabe's mix.

Tom Schnabel, the first music director and host of public radio station KCRW's long-running show *Morning Becomes Eclectic*, was happy to see McCabe's stretch out over the years: "I'm not a big folkie, but I loved seeing Ry Cooder there with Ali Farka Toure and Hamza El Din, the great oud master. Ditto for kora master Toumani Diabate and [tabla player] Zakir Hussain. The Moroccan gnawa trance music of Hassan Hakmoun, and the Tuvan throat singer Huun-Huur Tu. Who else would book those artists? It occupies a rare niche in the L.A. music scene."

In 1981, when Louie Perez saw that Tex-Mex music legend Flaco Jiménez was performing at McCabe's, he called Nancy Covey with hopes that she would book his band to open the show. When he introduced himself as Louie of Los Lobos del Este De Los Angeles, there was silence on the other end of the line. Nancy had never heard of this band—and Louie was not surprised.

While attending Garfield High School in East Los Angeles in 1973, Louie, a percussionist, and his friend, guitarist/accordionist David Hidalgo, recruited guitarist Cesar Rosas and bassist Conrad Lozano to start a band that fused blues, rock 'n' roll, jazz, and doo-wop with the traditional Mexican and Latin American music they had grown up with.

They soon added multi-instrumentalist Steve Berlin. And after honing their chops at backyard family parties, weddings, and Mexican restaurants, in 1978, the band recorded and released their first album, *Los Lobos del Este De Los Angeles (Just Another Band from East LA)*, and they slowly started to make a name for themselves. It was a name that had not quite made its way to Nancy, so she was unsure until Louie explained that they would play for free just for the honor of opening for one of their heroes. So, Los Lobos, as they would eventually come to be known, opened the two shows and familiarized themselves with Flaco and the rest of the band that included Ry Cooder, as well as the McCabe's audience. The band would return to headline two shows in 1984, just prior to the release of the soundtrack of *La Bamba*, the biopic about rock 'n' roller Ritchie Valens in which the group was featured. The film catapulted Los Lobos to international stardom, earning them industry recognition and a Grammy Award. While this caused them to outgrow McCabe's, individual band members return to the stage in various combinations over the years, and the full band took part in McCabe's fiftieth anniversary concert in 2008.

The occasion also created a lifelong friendship between Los Lobos and Nancy Covey, and they attended and performed at her wedding.

In 1979, jazz journalist Kirk Silsbee was pleasantly surprised to receive a notice that vocalist and pianist Blossom Dearie was set to appear at the venue. He said, "McCabe's gave jazz musicians what they always said they wanted, which was attentive audiences in a recital space."

Although guitarists like Kenny Burrell, Les Paul, Herb Ellis, and Joe Pass had performed at McCabe's earlier in the 1970s, jazz had now become more of a regular feature at the shop. Finding that audiences were happy to come to hear jazz in an intimate venue without the distractions of a bar and food servers milling about, luminaries like Les McCann, Jon Hendricks, Mose Allison, John Abercrombie, McCoy Tyner, Randy Weston, Frank Morgan, Dewey Redman, Jack DeJohnette, Gary Peacock, Don Cherry, Gary Burton, Dave Holland, Paul Horn, and the Manhattan Transfer began playing live at McCabe's Guitar Shop.

Kirk recalled an unusual evening when he went to see the guitarist Bill Frisell: "I got a real kick out of him." Bill passed out photocopied sheets of the lyrics for the "The Ballad of Davy Crockett" and led that audience in a sixteen-chorus sing-along to the 1950s classic "and then invited Nels Cline up for guitar duets," according to Kirk.

It wasn't the first time Nels Cline had been to the shop. He said, "I likely became aware of McCabe's because I grew up about a five-minute drive from there, and the grocery store that my mother frequented was practically across the street. My brother Alex and I really enjoyed going to that market with her to visit with Ray, the butcher, and to hit the drugstore that was on the corner to get Marvel comic books. The McCabe's sign was quite noticeable!"

Nels formed a teenage rock band called Homogenized Goo and then gravitated toward jazz. He was in the McCabe's audience quite often, taking full advantage of the musical diversity the shop offered, including concerts by Pat Metheny, Henry Kaiser and Fred Frith, Cat Power, Richard Thompson, Lenny Breau, George Winston, Will Ackerman, Alex DeGrassi, Mose Allison, and fIREHOSE to name a few.

Three concerts really stand out in his memory:

> *One was the band Oregon, of whom I was fanatically fond. I guess the sad little spinet piano was unacceptable to Ralph Towner/their management,*

because they had a rented baby grand for those sets. Of course, it wouldn't fit on the stage along with the band members, so it was on the floor in front of the stage, which meant sacrificing maybe ten seats. That back room is so small that shrinking its capacity was a real sacrifice!

Second, I got to hear the brilliant guitar legend Ted Greene play solo guitar. It was right when his album Guitar Solos *had been released, and he was mesmerizing. His harmonic inventiveness, harp-like artificial harmonics, and crystalline tone resonate in my memory to this day. Who knew that he would end up performing in public so rarely?*

Third, I went to hear Howard Roberts play jazz tunes in a quartet, and his be-bop playing was just jaw-dropping. My brother Alex and I sat in the first row right in front of Howard. I don't recall who was in Howard's band, but the opening act was extremely memorable. As the band went into an extremely soft bossa nova groove, this singer took gum out of his mouth and dropped it into a glass of water then started to sing "You Are the Sunshine of My Life" at a whisper as he sort of writhed around sensuously. It was Al Jarreau! His first record was about to be released, and he was backed by Tom Canning (who played keys with Al for decades), Wolfgang Melz, and…Joey Baron! Joey is so memorable looking behind the drums that when we finally met at Bill Frisell band shows, Alex and I remembered him, his big smile, his posture, from that Al Jarreau set!

Nels himself first performed at McCabe's in 1981 in a duet with bassist Eric Von Essen, opening for saxophonist Joe Farrell and bassist Charlie Haden.

One of the most revolutionary bassists in the history of jazz, Charlie Haden, was a regular presence on the McCabe's stage in the early 1980s while he was living in Los Angeles. An original member of the groundbreaking Ornette Coleman Quartet and a member of Keith Jarrett's various ensembles, Charlie also formed his own bands, Quartet West and the Liberation Music Orchestra.

Kirk Silsbee recalled that Charlie was a real charmer: "Charlie hadn't been in L.A. too long when my phone rang one day. 'Hey man, it's Charlie Haden.' You could have knocked me over with a feather. 'I've got this gig coming up, and it sure would be great if someone could write a 'Critic's Choice' about it.' So, of course I did. He was not shy about asking favors from anyone."

Charlie would soon befriend Nancy Covey's assistant, John Chelew, and would return to the venue time and again once John took over booking duties for McCabe's Guitar Shop. He played concerts with Don Cherry, Billy Higgins, and Ginger Baker, among others. Nels Cline also played the McCabe's stage a number of times before he was invited to join the alternative rock band Wilco.

PHOTO GALLERY

Ellen Griffith

Ellen Griffith, whose children Sue and Wayne both worked at McCabe's, started taking photographs at the shop in the 1970s. A statement on her website reads:

> *I had a wandering ear for all forms of roots music, and I subsequently strayed into blues, folk music, and bluegrass. To me, it was all related—where there's a heartbeat rhythm that feels like it came from the lives of real folks. I guess it's organic. Much of my misspent youth was consumed with collecting old 78- and 45-RPM records. Why? In a pre-internet world, the dusty grooves of old wax and vinyl were the only clues to the roots of our American music. All those valuable sounds of history are now on YouTube…if you know where to look. Some were more influential than they were popular. But they all have a story to tell.*

The following photos were taken by Ellen Griffith, www.recallmusic.com, and provided by her family.

Dave Van Ronk.

Doc Watson.

John Lee Hooker.

Above: Bill Monroe.

Left: Elizabeth Cotten.

Roosevelt Sykes.

Mike Bloomfield.

Willie Dixon (*left*) with Nancy Covey (*right*).

Elizabeth Cotten (*left*) with Nancy Covey (*right*).

Gene Clark (*left*) and Roger McGuinn (*right*).

Sippie Wallace (*left*) and Bonnie Raitt (*right*).

From left to right: Roy Brown, Big Mama Thornton, and Pee Wee Clayton.

Mike Bloomfield.

Brownie McGhee (*left*) and Sonny Terry (*right*).

Doc Watson (*left*) and Dave Van Ronk (*right*).

Warren Zevon (*left*) and T Bone Burnett (*right*).

Above: *Left to right*: Roger McGuinn, Richard Thompson, and T Bone Burnett.

Right: Elvis Costello (*left*) and John Hiatt (*right*).

15
THE TAKOMA CONNECTION

About a year after Gerald McCabe opened the guitar shop on the West Coast, guitarist John Fahey started his own record label on the East Coast. Named after his hometown of Takoma Park, Maryland, Takoma's first release was John's album of original steel string guitar solos titled *Blind Joe Death*. When John moved to Berkeley, California, in 1960, he hooked up with ED Denson, who was then managing the folk rock band Country Joe and the Fish. ED took over operations at Takoma. The label released more albums by John, as well as other instrumentalists who were influenced by his self-proclaimed "primitive guitar" style. The label got a major boost in 1969 after the release of the album *6 and 12 String Guitar* by Leo Kottke, which remains Takoma's bestseller.

Then John relocated to Los Angeles in 1970 to get his master's degree at UCLA, and he put Takoma in the hands of his wife, Jan. Jon Monday, who had recently arrived in Venice, California, from the San Francisco Bay Area, where he had operated a psychedelic light show company, was hired to do mailings three days a week for four hours a day. With a weekly salary of fifty dollars, he soon left and did odd jobs for a while, awaiting his next opportunity in the music business.

One of Jon's friends was the West Coast promotion director for a major label who asked him to help with mailing albums to reviewers and music directors. When Jon observed how this practice helped promote sales and airplay, he went back to John Fahey and pitched the idea of doing the same for Takoma.

Jon Monday recalled:

> *He* [John Fahey] *hired me to do that as Takoma's first full-time employee. I'd go on the road with him occasionally to do local marketing and promotion when Fahey was playing. Jan was running the company. In the summer of 1971, I went on a big U.S. tour with Fahey, and on that trip, he told me he was divorcing Jan and asked if a mutual friend, Charlie Mitchell, would be good to take over running the company as president. I agreed.*
>
> *When Charlie took over, he began looking for a new place for the office, as we were growing and now were three employees—Charlie, me, and Carol the bookkeeper. We looked at several places but settled on an office that was right next door to McCabe's.*

Although the Takoma office was right next door to the shop, booking John Fahey to play at McCabe's was not as easy as it seemed. Bobby Kimmel recalled, "I went next door one time when he was at Takoma and asked him to play McCabe's." John Fahey's response: "He took off his pants in front of me, put on his swimming trunks, and said, 'I'm going to the beach.'"

However, John went on to play McCabe's on numerous occasions.

Kirk Silsbee, who became a music journalist for the *Los Angeles Reader*, first came to McCabe's as a teenager to see an afternoon concert by John

Jon Monday in the Takoma Studio. *Photo provided by Jon Monday.*

Fahey in 1971. "Fahey made little or no concession to presentation. He just sat up there, tuning his twelve-string endlessly, not relating to the audience, every now and then giving a title while working his way through a six-pack of Coca-Cola. He would play these wonderful guitar fantasias that just started out of nowhere and eventually crashed to the ground after ten or so minutes." Once the show was over, Kirk spent some time browsing in the store: "I'm dazzled by these stringed instruments and the guitar instruction books, and I'm poking around a little bit. And I open a door, and it turns out to be a janitor's closet.…And in the closet is Fahey with a tortoise that he's holding.…And he doesn't say anything but looks at me with those Fahey owl eyes as if to say, What's the matter with you, baby?'" Kirk closed the door and "let it go at that."

Guitarist Nels Cline recalled going to see John Fahey with their mutual friend George Winston:

> *George had known Fahey for some time and had recorded his first record, Piano Solos, for Takoma. I met George when he came into the record store where I worked—Rhino Records—and he eventually asked me (I was the used and cut-out jazz person there then) whether he could buy multiple copies of his Takoma album, which we had many cut-out copies of (and which few, if any, were bought at that time). I had only seen Fahey "live" once before, and I was psyched that I would likely finally meet him after the show. It turned out that Fahey was quite ill with some kind of virus. He was drinking a pitcher of beer (McCabe's famously did not serve alcohol, so someone got it for him somehow) and was sweating profusely. He was quite candid about how awful he felt and mentioned it several times as I recall. Anyway, George decided that he should drive Fahey's car to make sure he got home OK and I should follow them. I can't recall whether I drove George's burnt-looking VW Bug or whether I drove my dirt-colored VW Squareback, but I followed Fahey and George to Fahey and his wife's place. I waited in the living room while George got Fahey safely into bed. I assumed that Fahey's wife was sound asleep and I never met her, nor did I have any substantive interaction with Fahey, but it was quite a memorable evening!*

While George Winston's self-defined "rural folk piano" style developed widespread audiences through his releases on the Windham Hill label in the 1980s, he was relatively unknown in 1977, having released only that one album. Consequently, when he made his own debut at McCabe's, he played to only a handful of people.

Soundman Alan Kanter recalled not having to work very long or hard that night: "George looked out at the audience and said, 'You know, I'm going to play one or two piano songs, and then why don't we all head out to the front room and I'll just sit down on the floor and play some guitar stuff for you.'" It was an intimate, unamplified treat for the few folks in attendance. George returned several times in the early '80s to play to full houses once his breakthrough album *Autumn* was released.

Jon Monday's work included producing and engineering, as well as art direction, promotion, sales, and marketing. He recalled: "Takoma was growing fast, with Kottke and Fahey being our best-selling, and doing a solid catalog business with other artists."

John Fahey and Leo Kottke were two of the "Takoma Seven," an elite fraternity of fingerstyle guitar virtuosos including Peter Lang, Robbie Basho, Toulouse Engelhardt, and Rick Ruskin, who were chosen to record for Takoma and their affiliates. All of them played at McCabe's on various occasions, either headlining or on bills with other artists.

Rick Ruskin first met John Fahey at McCabe's "by almost stepping on him, as he was prone on the floor in front of the cash register desk.... To say he was eccentric is an understatement." Rick recorded three albums for Takoma and worked with John on his second Christmas album, arranging all the duets. He recalled that once they were in the studio, rehearsals were a bit odd, because he never knew which John Fahey he'd be dealing with—the personable one or the thorny one. Rick performed at McCabe's a dozen times between 1970 and 1973 and also gave lessons at the store.

Toulouse Engelhardt grew up in Southern California, influenced by the sound of the region's surf music, but he was soon exploring the instrument's infinite possibilities by taking lessons from jazz guitar icons Larry Carlton and Wes Montgomery. He also discovered McCabe's Guitar Shop: "In the summer of '75, I decided to attend a concert down at McCabe's to hear one of my guitar heroes Merle Travis. In my company that evening, on our first date, was a very special lady indeed, a ballerina who performed as an understudy with the Royal Ballet in the UK. After the show, she turned to me and said, 'Are you that good?' And I said, 'Nobody is that good!'"

Little did Toulouse know that a year later, almost to the day, he would be giving his debut performance on that very stage—and he would end up marrying his McCabe's date a few years after that.

He also didn't know how nervous his idol was before he took the stage. While retail manager Jack MacKenzie has a memory of Merle "walking through the front door, having a look around, and saying, 'Let's pick,'"

Wayne Griffith, who was working on the concert staff that night recalled, "I walked into the dressing room, and he was looking kind of worried." When Wayne asked the guitar legend if he was OK, Merle replied, "In this place, I know that every single person in the first five rows are guitar players, sitting there, watching exactly what I do."

Perhaps the only person who was more nervous than Merle was the guitarist opening the show that night, Happy Traum. Harry "Happy" Traum began playing guitar and banjo as an active participant in the legendary Washington Square/Greenwich Village scene of the 1950s and '60s. He studied guitar with the famed blues master Brownie McGhee and performed and recorded with the folk music ensemble the New World Singers. After moving to Woodstock, New York, in 1967, Happy started playing in a duo with his brother Artie and, along with his wife, Jane, created Homespun Tapes, which grew to include catalog of more than five hundred lessons in folk, blues, bluegrass, swing, old-time country, and jazz taught by musicians at the top of their field. Including CDs, DVDs, books, and downloads, Homespun Tapes are distributed and sold around the globe.

The Traums often spent the winter months in Santa Monica, and Happy played at McCabe's on many occasions. In a post on his website, he shared the following recollection of his initiation:

> *In 1975, I played my first of many gigs at McCabe's Guitar Shop, a legendary venue in Santa Monica, California. This was a very exciting event for me, mainly because I was opening for one of my all-time favorite guitarists, the great Merle Travis.*
>
> *When I went in for the soundcheck, I was, of course, quite nervous about meeting my hero. I walked into the room, and there was Merle, standing on stage looking like a million bucks. He was wearing snakeskin cowboy boots, a sequin jacket, and was wearing a big Stetson hat. He was holding his famous Bigsby guitar, with "Merle Travis" written in bold mother of pearl inlay up and down the fretboard.*
>
> *When his soundcheck was finished and before I started mine, I got up all my courage and nervously went up on the stage to introduce myself to him. I stuck out my hand and said, "Merle, it's a great honor for me to meet you. I've been a hero of yours for years!" I realized immediately that I said something that wasn't quite right but couldn't quite figure out how to correct myself. He just looked at me with a twinkle in his eye, shook my hand, and said, "Well, Happy, I've been a hero of yours for years as well." We both had a good laugh at that.*

Merle Travis. *Photo by Ellen Griffith.*

Happy Traum (*left*) performs at McCabe's with Jim Kweskin (*right*) decades after opening for Merle Travis. *Photo by Jane Traum, Homespun Tapes, www.homespun.com.*

A year before Toulouse Englehardt attended the Merle Travis concert, he recorded a number of his compositions, and his producer, songsmith and musician Chris Darrow of Kaleidoscope and Nitty Gritty Dirt Band fame, submitted the tapes to John Fahey to see if he would consider releasing the album on Takoma.

Toulouse recalled:

> *We brought the tapes back to L.A. and got Fahey's personal engineer Doug Decker to mix and master what eventually became* Toullusions. *At first, Fahey turned a cold shoulder to the tapes and called me the "Guitar Speiler" (German for "fast talker"), but the next day, after another listening, he agreed to release the album for distribution. I still have the crazy handwritten notes he wrote me, criticizing and then praising the music all in the same letter! In the end, I realized that as complex as his personality was, he was just trying to guide me along as a mentor as my career began to build momentum. "You're the next gunslinger to be tossed into the OK Corral, Toulouse, so here is what you need to do!"*

In 1976, just weeks after Takoma, in affiliation with Sierra/Briar Records, announced the release of the album, Toulouse was booked to play McCabe's. This turned out be a memorable—and, to some, infamous—performance, with shades of the 1965 Newport Folk Festival, when Bob Dylan went electric. Toulouse recalled:

> *Halfway through my instrumental set, I put down my twelve-string acoustic guitar and picked up a Mosrite "Ventures Model" electric guitar and began performing a series of comically ragtime "toons" smothered in reverb to the gasps of the audience. It was a naive move on my part, not realizing that I was breaking a sacred taboo in a strictly acoustic venue, but the move was an integral part of my performance, and these funny "toons" were featured on my new release* Toullusions.
>
> *The club manager at the time was furious and went ballistic over all this! After my performance and a second standing ovation, she came storming into the green room and wagged her finger in my face and exclaimed, "I don't care how good you are, you are never playing here again!" I was dumbfounded! Of course, that turned out not to be the case. After there was a change in management years later, I returned to the club on a few occasions to perform to a full house, and I believe everyone had a splendid time! Maybe it really was an honor to be the first artist to be "blacklisted" from performing at McCabe's Guitar Shop!*

Acoustic Toulouse. *Photo provided by Toulouse Engelhardt.*

Electric Toulouse. *Photo provided by Toulouse Engelhardt.*

Right around the time that McCabe's went electric, Takoma started working with the Tascam Audio System of America (TASCAM), which supplied the company with a sixteen-track recorder and mixing board that they took on the road to record a bluegrass festival.

Jon Monday recalled, "It was during that time I had the idea to connect the McCabe's sound booth to our office, where we could build a recording studio. We laid the cables—sixteen-pair mic cables and a coax video cable—[that] ended in a storage room, and we just did a stereo tape recording."

It wasn't long before those at Takoma had the idea of recording live concerts at McCabe's and releasing them on their fast-growing label.

16
LIVE AT McCABE'S

The first album to be recorded live at McCabe's was that of multi-instrumentalist Norman Blake, who spent the 1960s as a session player for Johnny Cash, Bob Dylan, Joan Baez, Kris Kristofferson, John Hartford, and many others. He subsequently launched his solo career, which showcased his formidable guitar prowess, putting the independent record labels Rounder and Flying Fish on the map in 1972 and 1974, respectively. Norman then signed with Takoma in 1976, and the label's engineer Doug Decker was brought in to capture his two-night stand at McCabe's in March that year.

Norman's awe-inspiring flat-picking was unleashed in the live setting at McCabe's, which elevated his stature as one of the top acoustic guitarists of the day. When he concluded the second track, "Sweet Heaven," with an extended, intricate coda, it's as if he couldn't stop improvising. Once the audience exploded with applause, Norman chuckled, "I don't know—you gotta cut me out of this thing." The recording includes much of Norman's patter between songs, as well as Nancy Covey's introduction, which adds to the live, in-the-moment feel of the album.

In his review on the *AllMusic* website, Jim Smith notes that the recording is one of the greatest flat-picking albums of all time, with Norman in his prime. He also remarks that the sound was marvelous.

Sam Bush, who has performed and recorded with Norman, agreed: "He would be a little more outgoing on stage and pull out the hot licks. That record got his flat-picking more noticed. I think that was the one that turned on a lot of good, young guitar players onto Norman's playing."

In appreciation of Norman Blake's legacy, bluegrass musician and educator Andy Bing, who runs Vassar College's continuing education program, *Bluegrass: Folk Music in Overdrive*, wrote:

> *Although Norman Blake is one of the best guitarists of his era, he has been careful to use his superb technique to make the song better, rather than to call attention to his technical flash. One possible exception, and boy is it fun to listen to, is* Live at McCabe's *from the 1970s, which captures Blake's friendly, relaxed manner and simply stupendous flat-picking. Listen to "Nine Pound Hammer." Maybe the energy from an adoring audience encouraged him to rear back and let the notes fly.*

Phil Gallo, who would become a journalist, covering music for *Variety*, *Billboard*, and *Hits Magazine*, was at the concert. As a teenager, he began playing acoustic bass and was in a band with older musicians playing bluegrass and old-time country music. His bandmates would often bring him to McCabe's in the mid-1970s to hear concerts.

Although Phil was not familiar with Norman Blake at the time, a friend of his was telling him, "You really gotta hear this guy." While he was impressed with Norman's technical and precise flat-picking skills, he was really taken with the duets he played with his musical partner, cellist Nancy Blake: "Once she joined him, the music had a whole other quality. To do fiddle tunes with a guitar and cello…that was the first time I had ever heard something like that." Phil did not know that the concert had been recorded, so he was elated when he saw the album at the record store. "Wait a minute—I was at that concert! I gotta buy this record!"

Guitar aficionado Maple Byrne noted, "That definitely was a trend-setter. I didn't see that show, but I definitely saw him and Nancy at McCabe's, which was a wonderful hillbilly chamber music kind of thing—totally unique."

Larry Campbell also spoke favorably of the album: "I've got it on vinyl! I saw it when it came out, and I said, 'OK, I'm buying this.' It was a wonderful record, and I was thrilled with the fact that it was recorded at McCabe's."

With the album design by Jon Monday, the album set a high bar for live acoustic music recordings and launched the "Live at McCabe's Guitar Shop" brand for Takoma.

Audio engineer Wayne Griffith was at the performance, although he did not mix the sound that night. He agreed it helped elevate McCabe's visibility outside of the Los Angeles area: "I have had more people comment on that show that come through here—mostly bluegrass people—that say that their first introduction to McCabe's was that record. That record has done a lot for McCabe's."

The original vinyl album was out of print for many years before a fan campaign brought about a reissue on the Fantasy label, which owned Takoma in the '90s.

As much as musicians and acoustic guitar aficionados revere the album, Norman himself does not consider it to be one of his favorite recordings. In an interview with *Bluegrass Unlimited*, he relayed that he was picking in an "OK-now-show-me-you-can-play" situation in which he was not particularly comfortable, and he felt that Takoma didn't really back up his music. Norman did record one more album for the label, *Directions*, this time in the Takoma studio, and not long after, he signed a multi-album deal with Rounder.

However, Norman returned to play live shows at McCabe's a number of times in subsequent years, and Takoma proceeded to release albums recorded at the guitar shop by Larry McNeely, Byron Berline & Sundance, and Maria Muldaur in the next few years.

Jon Monday recalled, "I made a deal with Bob Riskin to use the name McCabe's for a per-album-sold royalty. Sadly, I learned much later that he was never paid. We also worked closely with Alan Kanter, the McCabe's sound guy, who was extremely helpful—even did some soldering for us and helped with the cable design and specs."

It wasn't long before other artists wanted to record their concerts at McCabe's and release them on their own labels. This brought the "Live at McCabe's Guitar Shop" stamp of approval to recordings by John Hammond, Country Gazette, Bert Jansch, Ted Hawkins, Townes Van Zandt, Ralph Stanley, Tom Paxton, Henry Rollins, Robin Williamson, Nancy Wilson (from Heart), Freedy Johnston, John Stewart, David Hatfield, Paul Siebel with David Bromberg, Lyle Ritz & Herb Ohta, Gene Clark and Carla Olson, and Shelby Lynne.

A bootleg Live at McCabe's recording of R.E.M has been in circulation since 1987.

In 1979, John Fahey sold Takoma to a joint venture between Chrysalis Records, music business attorney Bill Coben, and producer/manager Denny Bruce.

In an article on the Cave Hollywood website, Denny Bruce recalls another historic album recorded at McCabe's.

Michael Bloomfield emerged as one of America's most electrifying blues guitarists through his recordings with the Paul Butterfield Blues Band and the Electric Flag, his "Super Session" and live albums with Al Kooper, and his memorable licks on Bob Dylan's *Highway 61 Revisited.* Once he moved to California, Mike played at McCabe's on several occasions and started recording for Takoma. His 1977 show at McCabe's, *I'm With You Always*, captures the extraordinary chops—on both acoustic and electric guitar—of one of the greatest American blues virtuosos.

Denny Bruce remembered that Michael had already done one album for Takoma and knew and liked how the company worked—no pressure at all on the artist, just record when you feel like it. He wanted to do a quiet, solo show in a small club doing all acoustic guitar and some piano songs. Michael was booked at McCabe's, and Denny thought it would be a nice room for a solo recording. When he called Michael the day before the gig to see what time the guitarist would be coming down from his home in Northern California, his answer was that he would be coming with Mark Naftalin, so a piano would be needed, and he'd already hooked up with a drummer and bass player who lived in Los Angeles.

When Denny said, "I thought you wanted to do a solo album." Mike responded, "I have trouble telling friends they can't play on this gig."

Denny described that just fitting this gear on the narrow McCabe's stage took skill, planning, and patience, but Michael did two sets and "got a good album out of it." In 2008, ten more songs from that weekend were released as *Mike Bloomfield: Live at McCabe's Workshop*. Selected tracks from the first release were also included in the 2014 comprehensive, career retrospective set, *From His Head to His Heart to His Hands*, released on Legacy/Sony Records.

Eventually, Chrysalis sold Takoma and brought Jon Monday into the main company as a utility player, reporting directly to the president and holding several positions, including director of marketing and sales manager of the video division.

When Marty Rifkin, a well-known session guitarist and record producer who worked in between gigs at McCabe's, selling guitars and giving lessons, was ready to open his own recording studio, he set his sights on the historic Takoma site, two doors down from McCabe's. Just prior to closing the deal, he was informed that the building's zoning had changed and would allow only retail use. Disappointed, Marty unsuccessfully tried to obtain a variance and subsequently landed about three miles west at the former rehearsal studio of the Beach Boys.

17
HOWL

In 1983, McCabe's stature as a premier listening room for folk, blues, bluegrass, roots rock, and jazz surged through Nancy Covey's diligence and creativity as curator, and the live albums helped take the venue's notoriety well beyond Southern California. Its stage size and audience capacity remained a challenge, so Nancy was still seeking ways to expand McCabe's reach. She thought spoken word performances held great potential for diversifying programming to bring new audiences through the doors. Nancy knew who to call.

Harvey Kubernik was a music journalist for the *Los Angeles Free Press*, and this led him to becoming a contributor to the British publication *Melody Maker*. He also served as the director of the Artists & Repertoire Department at MCA Records. Harvey had a particular affinity for the Beat Generation of writers and poets, who were often inspired by jazz. Artists of this generation included Jack Kerouac and Allen Ginsberg, whose books, *On the Road* and *Howl (and Other Poems)*, respectively, became synonymous with the counterculture movement that emerged in the 1950s.

Harvey had a vision for creating nationally touring performances that would combine his various interests, and he began putting together events at Los Angeles's Lhasa Club. He was subsequently invited to produce the spoken word/poetry segments for the *I.R.S. Records Presents: The Cutting Edge* music program that was broadcast monthly on MTV. "You couldn't call what I do a career—it's an improv jazz life," he said. "I'm coming from multi-disciplinary mixed media world, including film, authors, dance. I was always into the words—the wordsmith thing."

Harvey especially liked the idea of working at McCabe's because it invited people of all ages: "I never got to see some music during the '60s because I was under eighteen or twenty-one." When Harvey first tried to reach out to McCabe's, he had trouble getting their attention, but he finally got a call from Nancy Covey: "I know you are putting on these shows. Why don't you come down as a guest of mine?" Harvey accepted, and then Nancy followed up with another invitation: "Why don't you put on a show here?" Again, Harvey happily accepted and did not waste any time bringing together iconic Beat poet Allen Ginsberg and rising psychobilly star Mojo Nixon for an evening at McCabe's in March 1983. Just as Bob Riskin gave all the concert directors complete autonomy when it came to choosing musicians, Nancy Covey gave Harvey free reign to put together his spoken word evenings. Harvey said, "Politics were never discussed. It was always just, 'What do you want to do?'"

Allen Ginsberg would go on to appear nearly a dozen times at McCabe's, and the monthly spoken word events would continue to include appearances by Michael McClure, Michael C. Ford, Linda Albertano, Randall Kennedy, Michelle T. Clinton, Ivan E. Roth, Daniel Sugerman, and Wanda Coleman, among others.

Allen Ginsberg (*left*) and Harvey Kubernik (*right*). *Photo provided by Harvey Kubernik.*

Right around the time Harvey started producing the spoken word series at McCabe's, he read interviews with punk rock singers Henry Rollins of Black Flag and Jello Biafra of the Dead Kennedys, and he had another idea. "Their interviews were so good—I knew that they could work on stage." Harvey approached both artists to see if they would consider putting together a performance of words without music, and they both agreed to it.

Living in Los Angeles, Henry Rollins had been to McCabe's to see a show by John Lee Hooker, but his spoken word performance, one of the first ones he ever performed, marked his debut on the stage. Henry recalled, "I immediately liked the venue. It was much different than places I played with the band I was in. Also, the audience was much friendlier than what I was used to. It was small, which I really liked. It was obvious McCabe's was all about music, performance, and seemed to be performer-oriented, which was a rare situation for me in those days."

Harvey helped arrange Henry's first U.S. solo tour, and after leaving Black Flag and then fronting the Rollins Band for several years, Henry started to exclusively tour with his spoken word format.

Cover of Henry Rollins *Live at McCabe's* recording. *Image provided by Henry Rollins.*

In 1990, Henry performed two shows at McCabe's along with Exene Cervenka and Hubert Selby Jr. These shows were recorded—as all shows at McCabe's were—and the tape was handed to Henry after the show. "They came out sounding pretty good, and I chose to put them out," he said. "There wasn't always a lot of planning in those days. I'd get an idea and just go for it."

The result was the album *Rollins: Live at McCabe's*.

While Henry outgrew McCabe's and started playing much larger venues across the country, he did return in 2018 as part of the store's sixtieth anniversary season. "It was great to see how little the place had changed and how great it was to be in that rare space again," he said. "McCabe's is absolutely part of the Southern California music scene story. It is a noble venue. It's part of the artistic-cultural conversation of Los Angeles. McCabe's should always be in operation."

Harvey Kubernik's series of spoken word events concluded in 1986 with a somewhat controversial performance by Native author, poet, actor, musician, and political activist John Trudell and the Dead Kennedys' Jello Biafra. "The room was packed for this game-changing uncensored verbal platform of Indian and punk tongue," Harvey recalled and said that there may have been complaints that this show was a bit too radical. At this point, Harvey moved his spoken word shows to Bebop Records and Fine Art in Reseda about fifteen miles northwest of Santa Monica.

When reflecting on his tenure producing spoken word events at McCabe's, Harvey feels that if he had been able to get the full support of public radio and some grant funding, he would have been able to further expand the offerings at McCabe's.

He did point out that the stature of the series could have been substantially elevated by the "one that got away": "I approached Leonard Cohen about doing a spoken word album at McCabe's…and it almost happened." When Harvey approached Leonard, with whom he was well acquainted through previous interviews, the iconic singer/songwriter who had penned such classics as "Suzanne" and "Hallelujah" and had actually started his career as a writer of poetry and novels, expressed interest. "I sought outside funding to finance it," Havey said, "but didn't get the green light."

Harvey had also hoped to produce an evening of spoken word with Laura Nyro, whose songs "Stoned Soul Picnic" and "When I Die" established her as one of the premiere songwriters of the 1960s and '70s. "I helped bring Laura Nyro into that room," recalled Harvey. When Laura was between labels, Harvey thought her songwriting process—which Laura herself described saying, "When I write music, I see all the rivers flowing…sensual, spiritual, religious, animal, intellectual"—lent itself to an evening of spoken word. However, Laura demurred, and she was yet another "one who got away."

Harvey's passion for words eventually led him to have a career as an author. He has written twenty books about music, including *Canyon of Dreams: The Magic and the Music of Laurel Canyon* and *Leonard Cohen: Everybody Knows*.

Los Angeles rock musician Greg Franco, who is a regular in the seats at McCabe's, sees Harvey as a significant force in the city's cultural landscape: "Harv is always ahead of the curve, but his intention always is prioritizing the art and the artist first, and that's a rare thing these days. To me, he's a national treasure. He deserves more recognition than he gets."

As much as Harvey worshipped the spoken word, he was equally immersed in Los Angeles's music scene, and he saw another possibility for stretching the boundaries of McCabe's programming. Similar to his concept of presenting spoken word performances by Henry Rollins and Jello Biafra, he envisioned that some of Los Angeles's punk rock frontmen could leave their bands behind and put their lyrics at the forefront with a stripped-down show for a listening audience. McCabe's was the perfect venue, and Peter Case was the ideal artist.

Peter Case grew up in Buffalo, New York, and played his songs at coffeehouses and dances. He left home at the age of sixteen and busked around New York City; Washington, D.C.; and Boston before he landed in San Francisco in 1973. There, Peter was the main subject of the film *Night Shift*, a piece about the city's street music scene. He next formed the rock band the Nerves and, in 1977, relocated to Los Angeles, where he began performing and promoting the city's first punk rock shows. The following year, he formed the Plimsouls, and the band released an album on Geffen Records.

On his nights off, Peter could often be found in the audience at McCabe's. Peter recalled:

> *The first time I went there was to see Sandy Bull and Bob Neuwirth play. I saw T Bone* [Burnett] *early in my McCabe's introduction. The show with Memphis Slim was incredible. I'd been listening to him since I was fifteen, and then to hear him up close like that and actually meet him after the show was a powerful experience. I sat right behind him as he played. Opening that night was a genius named Henry Butler…one of the unsung greats of piano…more jazz and gospel than blues, but he could play anything and did. Dave Van Ronk's shows there were always special. I loved him so much. Doc Watson was great, and I got to meet him upstairs after the show and we had a very interesting talk.*

As a result of experiencing the traditional blues and folk music presented at McCabe's, Peter began to rediscover his own roots. He flipped the switch from electric to acoustic, and by 1984, he was ready to premiere his new sound at McCabe's. He said, "That was the first one, booked by Nancy Covey at the instigation of Harvey Kubernik. That was the first show of my solo career. It went down great.…The shows were sold out, but I was over-the-top nervous. It was more intense to play McCabe's than a lot of the big rock 'n' roll festivals and clubs I'd been paying with the Souls.…At McCabe's, you *knew* they were listening."

After his McCabe's debut, Peter indeed became comfortable playing in the intimacy of the shop, where he has since played dozens of times—likely more than any other musician. And it wasn't long before others started to join him on stage. "Bob Neuwirth came along on one of these gigs, and we did a thing where I sang in French and he translated," he said. "It was a joke, and at one point, Bob couldn't stop laughing—he just lost it." He recalled another night when his guests included T Bone Burnett and Steven Soles on guitar, Bonnie Raitt on piano, and Micky Raphael on harmonica. "It was pretty magical."

Then, when the Plimsouls reunited in 1995, they played two nights at McCabe's. Peter has been present for a number of McCabe's milestones—the all-star fiftieth anniversary concert at Royce Hall and a sixtieth anniversary show with Dave Alvin and Syd Straw—and he even celebrated his own sixtieth birthday with a concert at the shop.

In 2009, Peter started a session of his popular songwriting class at McCabe's before a planned tour of the UK and parts of Europe. However, the tour did not happen. Instead, Peter found himself in the hospital having unexpected double bypass surgery. He successfully recovered—but with a tall stack of hospital bills. In true McCabe's-to-the-rescue fashion, T Bone Burnett, Dave Alvin, Carla Olson, Stan Ridgway, Syd Straw, Phranc, Van Dyke Parks, Loudon Wainwright III, Richard Thompson, and Bob Neuwirth joined forces to stage three nights of fundraising concerts.

The 2023 documentary film *A Million Miles Away*, a piece about Peter's musical journey, begins with him in concert at McCabe's. "Since I played my first modern-era solo gig there in 1984, I've always considered it my 'home club,' the venue in the world I feel most comfortable in," he said.

18
OUT WITH A *BANG*

By 1984, Nancy was spending a fair amount of time away from California, either in England with Richard Thompson or off leading groups on Festival Tours, and she was also developing a documentary for PBS about Elizabeth Cotten. Realizing "I had done what I set out to do," she decided to leave McCabe's—but not too quietly.

Her planned departure coincided with her tenth anniversary of working at McCabe's, and she used the two milestones to stage a party. "I officially booked Richard [Thompson], Jennifer Warnes, Van Dyke Parks, John Hiatt and T Bone Burnett," she said. However, when word about the occasion got out, Jackson Browne, David Lindley, and Nicolette Larsen also decided to stop by. For his set, T Bone was accompanied by Ry Cooder, and he also invited his friend Warren Zevon on stage to perform a couple of tunes, including his classic "Lawyers, Guns and Money."

Charles Andrews, a music journalist who had moved to Santa Monica from Albuquerque, was the nightclub advertising rep for the *LA Weekly* at that time, and he went to McCabe's regularly. When he heard about the announced lineup for Nancy's farewell bash, he called to request a press pass. Charles recalled Nancy saying, "'Look, everyone in the world wants to be here for that....I may have to put you in the sound room.' I said, 'That's OK!'" As it turns out, Charles ended up watching the show in the hallway just outside the sound room, close to the steps that lead from the artists' dressing room to the stage. "We were packed in like sardines," he said. "I'm sure it was totally against all fire regulations. But all of a sudden, there's a jostling of the crowd, and I look over and I think, 'Who in the hell is trying to get closer?' None of us can move, and I look over and there's Elvis Costello, making his way through the crowd. And he goes up on the stage, plugs in his guitar."

Elvis and T Bone, who had recently started appearing as the Coward Brothers, performed "Ragged but Right" and then were joined by John Hiatt to play John's recently recorded "She Loves the Jerk" and the George Jones gem "She Thinks I Still Care." Then Elvis sang another country classic, "Why Don't You Love Me (Like You Used to Do)," and Jackson took the mic for "Twist and Shout" before passing it along to Warren for "Werewolves of London."

From the stage, Richard Thompson remembered: "The lucky audience were treated to an amazing evening, and the guests kept coming. When Elvis Costello walked on at the end, I swear a couple of people in the front row actually fainted."

Charles Andrews recalled that the audience was still in a little bit of disbelief about what they were witnessing and didn't have much time to soak it all in when, after a brief pause, Elvis stepped "forthrightly up to the microphone and started to sing, 'So you want to be a Rock and Roll Star.' And everybody on stage just grinned and joined right in."

Nancy took the stage to a thunderous ovation, for both the astounding show they had just experienced and for her game changing decade as McCabe's concert director. When the applause finally subsided, Nancy said, "I don't think I can top that. I'm retiring!" She then thanked her assistant, Tracy Strann; her predecessor, Bobby Kimmel; and "John Chelew…who's next…good luck."

19

IN WITH A *BOOM*

Turns out, John Chelew did have good luck. He had the good fortune of being able to book a venue that now had a well-established reputation as a go-to stage for folk, blues, bluegrass, country, roots rock, and jazz musicians, built by Bobby Kimmel and Nancy Covey. He also inherited a relationship with producer Harvey Kubernik for spoken word events. But John also had eclectic musical tastes and had his own adventurous vision for expanding the programming at McCabe's Guitar Shop.

Wayne Griffith, who has worked with all the concert directors who came before and after and became one himself, reflected, "John Chelew was amazing. He had his finger on the pulse of this town. Under John, we had PJ Harvey, Beck, Suzanne Vega, Liz Phair, the Cowboy Junkies. It was a big change in the direction. It brought new people into McCabe's."

Steve Hochman, who attended concerts on a regular basis, starting with the legendary debut of Richard Thompson, began writing about music for the *Los Angeles Times* in 1985. He became a "professional McCabe's goer," writing reviews and feature stories about John Stewart, Martin Carthy, John Fahey, and others. He recalled getting to know the concert director really well. "John had some crazy ideas," he said. "Some would work, and some wouldn't work. He was always excited about the things that could be happening there."

Rock musician Zachariah Love, who had become friendly with John Chelew, was eventually hired as his assistant and then succeeded him as concert director, reflected, "It was really John Chelew who brought the scope of what McCabe's was offering…and opened it up to a wider variety of performers. I was endeavoring to keep that going when I took over for John."

Lincoln Myerson, who succeeded Zach as concert director, was also heavily influenced by John's artistic vision: "John Chelew's legacy was that he really expanded the vocabulary of the music that McCabe's was presenting. One of the legendary stories is that a young Dwight Yoakum played his first shows at McCabe's when he opened a weekend, the first night for the [punk rock band] Meat Puppets, and the second night for [bluegrass legend] Bill Monroe."

No doubt, John had his eye on putting together concerts that would bring together some of Los Angeles's cutting-edge musicians, and he was determined to not be limited by genre, stage size, or decibel level.

Likely, one of the most epic and memorable performances in McCabe's history took place on September 22, 1984, just a few months after John took the helm. It was a double bill of jazz bassist Charlie Haden's Liberation Music Orchestra and the hardcore rock band the Minutemen, featuring guitarist/vocalist D. Boon, bassist/vocalist Mike Watt, and drummer George Hurley.

Guitarist Nels Cline was there:

> *Yes, that Liberation Music Orchestra (LMO)/Minutemen concert really happened! I was playing with LMO and was also a big fan of the Minutemen. Charlie showed up super late for soundcheck, and the band—about twelve to thirteen musicians—waited for quite some time for Charlie to arrive with all the charts so we could soundcheck and get off the stage for the Minutemen. The McCabe's stage was quite small, so this was pretty crazy.*
>
> *I was actually the person who put Joe Carducci from SST Records in touch with Charlie. He called me at the record store. Charlie's son Josh was inspired by* [Minutemen bassist] *Mike Watt to play bass, and he had a punk band then called the Treacherous Jaywalkers who had an album out on the Minutemen's label, New Alliance. As such, Charlie was quite aware of the Minutemen, and I know he dug them both musically and politically. In a way, the whole event was devised as a kind of gift to Josh, who sat in the front row with his mother, Ellen, and his triplet sisters, Tanya, Rachel, and Petra, who were maybe about eleven years old then.*
>
> *This day was the only time I spoke with D. Boon. As the Minutemen were sitting together waiting, I walked up to them and asked, "Are you guys going to play 'West Germany' tonight?" They looked at each other*

The Minutemen with Charlie Haden. *Left to right*: D. Boon (guitar), George Hurley (drums), Charlie Haden (acoustic bass), and Mike Watt (electric bass). *Photo by Dennis Keeley, www.denniskeeleyphoto.com.*

quizzically. "This guy who plays nylon-string guitar with Charlie Haden knows our music?" And eventually, D. Boon said, "Maybe."

Charlie famously sat in with them that night on a free improv sort of thing, and as I recall, he went into his "John Henry" riffs that he was so fond of during it. It was a really exciting night for me. And who could have known that ten years later, I would record and tour with Mike Watt?

20
HOMETOWN HEROES

John Chelew's interest in exposing the extraordinary talent that was available right in McCabe's fertile Los Angeles backyard became evident soon after he took charge of booking the shop's the series.

Louisiana-born Lucinda Williams had recorded a pair of albums for Folkways before moving to the Silver Lake neighborhood in Los Angeles in 1984, and it wasn't long before she heard about the guitar store that presented concerts in Santa Monica. "I was meeting other musicians, and the name McCabe's would pop up in a conversation," she said. "People would talk about it or say they were performing there. It was a pretty popular place. It was the best of the best of folk, blues, and Americana."

Lucinda soon met John Chelew, and she credits him with being "the one to give me a chance there, bringing me into McCabe's and making all that happen. He was very open and helpful. L.A. was really good to me. And I was meeting all kinds of creative people, and John Chelew was one of them. We had something in common because we all loved Bert Jansch, and Pentangle, and Nick Drake, and all that English arty folk stuff, so we bonded through that."

To expose the audiences at McCabe's to Lucinda's music, John booked her three days in a row in September 1984—two concerts opening for Doc Watson and one in the middle supporting Cajun accordionist and singer Jo-El Sonnier.

Lucinda recalled her first time walking on the stage at McCabe's:

> *When I very first started playing at McCabe's, it was kind of scary because you're so close to people in the audience...everybody's really quiet...drinking coffee and tea....It was not like a rambunctious dive bar. You have to sort of regroup yourself into this other frame of mind because everybody's paying such strict attention to you. This* [was] *where I could see legendary folk singers whose records I listened to back in the '60s, like Geoff Muldaur. I had all of his records and listened to them all the time. I always felt really, really shy playing at McCabe's. It was like an honor to play there....It kind of held this notoriety about it....It was kind of a big deal.*

Lucinda met T Bone Burnett, as well as his guitarist David Mansfield and his bassist David Miner, at McCabe's: "They were kind of a part of that McCabe's scene." Lucinda ended up playing with the Davids on a regular basis. "I would just sing acoustically, and they would back me up. And that was one of the best experiences I ever had working with other musicians. They were just so sensitive and open to what I was doing. They just really got me."

Lucinda returned in 1986 to open a show by John Hiatt, and when she released her self-titled album on Rough Trade Records in 1988, she headlined at McCabe's three times that year, on bills with Rosie Flores, Jim Lauderdale, and David Halley. Lucinda took the stage again in 1991, but her release of the acclaimed album *Sweet Old World* in 1992 and the 1998 career-changing *Car Wheels on a Gravel Road* propelled Lucinda into much larger performance venues.

Seventeen Grammy nominations, including three wins, followed, and Lucinda was named "America's Best Songwriter" by *TIME* magazine in 2002.

Then in 2018, Lucinda and her manager, Tom Overby, realizing they hadn't toured through Los Angeles that much, had the idea of booking a "World Tour of LA." As the tour centered on Lucinda playing intimate venues around the region, it included a two-night stand at McCabe's. "It kind of felt like coming back home," Lucinda said. "That whole McCabe's world was a safe, comfortable place to be."

John Chelew also expanded on the initiative that Nancy Covey and Harvey Kubernik had first implemented with Peter Case and invited some of Los Angeles's singer/songwriters who typically played in electric rock bands to play their music solo and acoustic.

Chris Difford and Glenn Tilbrook (Squeeze), Black Francis (the Pixies), John Doe (X), and Peter Himmelman (Sussman Lawrence) were just a few artists who left their bands at home and played acoustic shows in the intimacy afforded by McCabe's Guitar Shop. Steve Wynn of the band Dream Syndicate also became a regular presence on the McCabe's stage.

Born in Santa Monica, Steve got his first guitar when he was nine. He recalled:

> [The guitar] *was a cheap one with impossibly high action and difficult to keep in tune—in other words, the perfect first guitar, almost like reverse training wheels on a bicycle. If you can make a barre chord on a guitar like that without too much buzzing, you're on your way. But once I had a few years under my belt and could save up enough for a better guitar, I went straight down the road to McCabe's (I was living near the corner of Pico and Sepulveda at the time) and bought a Yamaha FG-140 that I still have today. It might have been the first time I walked into McCabe's, but* [it was] *most certainly not the last. I would drop by throughout high school in the mid to late '70s to get strings, look at sheet music, and ponder my next dream guitar.*

Steve formed the alternative rock band Dream Syndicate in 1981, and they quickly established themselves with the release of the albums *Days of Wine and Roses* and *Medicine Show*. Steve said:

> *In the meantime, not long after forming the Dream Syndicate, I began playing a few solo acoustic shows here and there. When John Chelew took over the booking of McCabe's, he approached me about playing a gig there. I was nervous as all get-out. I had a little flask of whiskey I would sip upstairs, which amused John no end. It did give me the courage, and John proceeded to book me there on a regular basis. I must have played over a dozen shows there in the late '80s—solo, with my acoustic trio, as part of other combos and even one night with the Dream Syndicate where I opened for myself, my solo acoustic quartet playing before the decidedly loud rock show of my main combo.*
>
> *I really credit McCabe's with me learning how to play solo acoustic shows. It was the perfect environment and one you don't get everywhere—a focused attentive audience, not distracted by noise, clinking drinks, bartenders, or an inebriated audience (although the buzz of the coffee and those delicious chocolate chip cookies is another story altogether; man, I would be positively wired when I hit the stage sometimes).*

One of my favorite memories there was a solo acoustic show I played, with my bandmates Chris Cacavas and Robert Lloyd in the audience. They came ostensibly as audience members, but at some point in the show, without introduction or announcement, [they] *pulled instruments—accordion and mandolin, respectively—from under their seats and just started playing along with me from the crowd—at first confusing and annoying and then delighting those around them, ultimately joining me on stage to finish the show.*

And then there's the famous 1987 show where I joined forces with R.E.M. and 10,000 Maniacs, Kendra Smith, Bob Forrest, and more for a pretty legendary show. In fact, I remember playing a show not long ago in Denmark where a girl up front was wearing a T-shirt that simply said "May 24, 1987." I asked after the show what the date meant, and she got all dreamy and glassy-eyed and said, "That's the date of your famous McCabe's show." It was a pretty amazing night, just a snowball of friends of various levels of fame all having fun and celebrating Texas Records, and mutual friends, and each other.

Once John stopped booking the club and I moved from L.A. to New York City, I didn't play McCabe's that often for a while. But I came back with the Baseball Project in 2014 [Peter Buck, Mike Mills, and Scott McCaughey]*—what a fun night. It had been a long time, and I was reminded of how much I loved playing there, even with a full rock band (and special guest Robert Lloyd) jammed onto the fabled tiny stage. I booked another show two years later with Robert, Mike Mills, and Linda Pitmon for an evening of "love songs" on Valentine's Day 2016. It's nice to be back in the McCabe's family, as I have been in one way or another for the last fifty years, and I hope many more to come.*

Another native Californian, Dave Alvin, grew up in Downey, twenty-five miles southeast of Santa Monica. He studied poetry in college and majored in creative writing, which eventually led to him becoming a songwriter.

Dave and his brother Phil, avid music fans since childhood, immersed themselves in vintage blues, country, and rockabilly sounds and often made the trek to the Ash Grove to see their heroes.

Dave recalled first visiting McCabe's in 1970, combining it with a visit to a nearby record shop called Jazzman Brown's, where the Alvin brothers would shop for old blues and jazz 78s and attend concerts by Kate Wolf, the Minutemen, and Peter Rowan in ensuing years.

In 1979, the brothers cofounded the Blasters, who built a strong following for their mix of roots rock and blues documented on a series of acclaimed recordings before Dave left to launch his solo career. As a side project, Dave also played guitar with the Knitters, who also included members of the rock band X.

However, his first appearance at McCabe's in 1984 did not highlight his musical chops; instead, it featured his poetry. "Harvey Kubernick put out these spoken word albums of musicians, and artists, and poets all reading their poems about Los Angeles or Southern California—he put that thing together," Dave said. It would be another five years before Dave played music on stage at McCabe's. In 1989, he played a show as the music director for singer/songwriter Syd Straw, who had just released her debut album, *Surprise*. "It was scary. It still is—playing at McCabe's is scary," Dave said. "People are listening—they're not drinking, they're not trying to dance. If one finger hits that fret the wrong way…it'll throw your whole night off. It is an intimidating stage."

Nevertheless, Dave started to perform his own music at McCabe's, and he credits the experience with his new career direction: "In the '80s, people from the noisier side of town were welcome into what was the quieter venue, and I think it really helped all of [the rock 'n' rollers who played there] develop as artists and become more well-rounded.…When you're playing the Whisky a Go Go, you're going to write a particular type of song that leans in a certain way as far as intensity, tempo, speed, volume." Once McCabe's became a regular haunt for Dave, he could see his elements and his approach to songwriting changing: "Chelew wasn't exactly comfortable with my voice because I was learning how to sing. I had never sung before in my life. I would get off stage, and John would give me these little pep talks—'You're almost there, man.' And he was right, as it wasn't until '94 that I really found my voice as a singer. But John still gave me shows there—he would overlook my problem with pitch—as the shows would sell out and we made money."

The songs Dave was workshopping at McCabe's that appeared on his 1994 album, *King of California*, proved to be a career turning point. The album became an Americana classic, and his newfound vocal style fit like a glove for the acoustic treatment of his repertoire. It also helped him gain a whole new following of roots music lovers.

The guitar shop ultimately became Dave's "clubhouse," and he performed there on a regular basis in a variety of combinations. Every January was reserved for Dave's mini-residency, and he would workshop his new songs: "McCabe's became part of my creative process."

In 1992, the Knitters reunited for a three-night stand, and in 1998, Dave performed two shows as part of the national "Monsters of Folk" tour, along with Tom Russell ("great goddam songwriter"), Chris Smither ("fantabulous guitar player"), and Ramblin Jack Elliott ("he's 'f—ing Ramblin' Jack Elliott").

Chris Smither, who emerged on the folk scene in Boston in the mid-'60s with Bonnie Raitt adopting his song "Love You Like A Man" and making it "Love Me Like A Man," which, in turn, brought his songwriting skills to the fore along with his finger-picking guitar virtuosity, remembers the McCabe's gig: "The Monsters tour was lots of fun, and I do remember that date. The small stage made things pretty cozy, but the place was packed, and everyone was playing well by that time.…I think it was the fourth of fifth show of the tour.…Ramblin' Jack was already getting tired, but the rest of us were just getting started.…Now I understand how he felt.… Years have given me perspective."

Chris has played McCabe's on a regular basis for decades. He said, "It's an inspiring place to play with a wonderful vibe.…I've never had a bad show there, and I always look forward to doing it."

While Dave and Phil Alvin had found initial success teaming up in rock band the Blasters, the brothers had a period, as the new millennium unfolded, in which they were not getting along very well. Anxious to make amends, Dave thought McCabe's could serve as a good place to reconnect. He called his brother: "Hey, Phil, I'm doing a couple of nights at McCabe's. Do you want to come down and sing a song or two?" Phil agreed, and the Alvin brothers performed together for the first time in ten years. "I have had a lot of emotional moments on that stage…and that was one of them."

As a result of the McCabe's reunion, Phil added his vocals to "What's Up with Your Brother" on Dave's next recording, which they followed up with two full albums they recorded together.

Dave also put together a memorable evening with Syd Straw and Peter Case to celebrate McCabe's Guitar Shop's sixtieth anniversary. And he curated a special concert to raise funds for Peter's medical bills following his double bypass surgery.

In 2020, Dave had his own health issues and received treatments that involved rounds of radiation and chemotherapy. As a result, he suffered from neuropathy (nerve damage caused by chemo) and was unable to play guitar for seven months. Dave had kept his situation to himself, and as he was recovering, he was unsure of his future in music.

Then in 2022, when Rick Holstrum, the guitarist for the Mavis Staples Band who had started a regular residency at McCabe's, asked Dave if he wanted to sit in. Dave agreed, and it proved to be his triumphant return to the stage: "It was wonderful. It was great. I said, 'OK I can do this.' Thank you, McCabe's!"

Although Dave now feels very much at ease in the venue where he had once said playing felt similar to performing naked, McCabe's storied history is still always in his mind when he takes the stage. "I won't say it's the Apollo Theatre or the Ryman Auditorium," he said, "but it's got that same kind of thing of 'Hey, John Stewart was on this stage'; 'Elizabeth Cotten was on this stage'; 'Doc Watson was on this stage.'…So you have something to live up to."

In his annual January residency in 2017, Dave sensed that the audience was on edge following the results of the 2016 presidential election, so he decided to end his show with a song he did not typically include in his repertoire because he felt it was a bit overdone—Woody Guthrie's "This Land Is Your Land." "But I felt we needed that song," he said. "I don't like to do sing-alongs—I'm not that kind of guy.…But I got everybody to sing along. It was really frigging moving. That was probably the most transcendental moment I had at McCabe's."

PHOTO GALLERY

John Casey

In 1986, JJ Cale—my elusive hero and pioneer of the "Tulsa sound"—was booked for two nights at McCabe's Guitar Shop, a place where strings and stories tangled in the air, where time didn't seem to matter. I wasn't going to miss this. I knew my way around a camera, so I made a call. My pitch was simple: I'd shoot both nights, develop the film, and frame the best shots in exchange for two tickets per show. John Chelew agreed, and just like that, I was in. JJ Cale didn't put on a show. He became the room. Every note, every pause, every word—it was all so deliberate, so real. And for those two nights, it felt like the world outside had been muted. It was just us, a small crowd in the back of a guitar shop, bearing witness to something that didn't need a name.

A collaboration was forming: I'd spot an act I wanted to shoot, John Chelew would nod. Then he'd suggest someone I didn't know, and I'd oblige. McCabe's wasn't just a music venue; it was a sanctuary, a vortex, pulling in talent and history, legends, and stories. These images, these stories—they're not just memories. They're proof that magic, once captured, never fades.

The following photos were taken by John Casey, Brown Dirt Music, www.curvedapocalypse.com.

Steve Earle.

JJ Cale.

David Lindley.

John Hiatt.

Lucinda Williams.

Taj Mahal.

Peter Rowan.

Timothy Leary.

21
OUT OF TOWN HEROES

As unplugged California rockers found a home at McCabe's, the stage continued to be a stop for out-of-town musicians touring the West Coast. While Guy Clark lived in Los Angeles for a short time in the early 1970s, his departure from the city is more famous. It was documented in his song "L.A. Freeway," which helped bring his extraordinary songwriting to the fore via the cover version by Jerry Jeff Walker.

Guy, who at one time opened up his own guitar repair shop and had a job building Dobros, went on to become known as the "king of Texas Troubadours," an elite group of singer/songwriters that included Townes Van Zandt, Steve Earle, Rodney Crowell, Jimmie Dale Gilmore, Joe Ely, Butch Hancock, and Kinky Friedman, all of whom took the stage in McCabe's back room.

In 1995, Townes released a *Live at McCabe's* album with a dozen tunes that included one of his most famous, "Pancho and Lefty." Guest appearances by Kelly Jo Phelps on Dobro and Barb Donovan on vocals, who joined him for his classic "I'll Be Here in the Morning," round out the set. The recording, like many of the "Live at McCabe's" albums, includes his between-song patter. At one point, Townes expresses, "If it gets any quieter in here, I'm going to give a sermon." He also muses, "You know, between here and the Santa Monica hotel across the way and the Mexican food restaurant up the street, you know if I ever retire."

Loudon Wainwright III also liked to frequent the aforementioned Mexican restaurant (Lares): "For people who played the room, that was the place to go and have Mexican food, margaritas, and get a little loose before the show."

There was a good chance that Townes went to Lares the night Dave Alvin went to see him and Guy Clark at McCabe's. Dave recalled, "I was a fan of Townes Van Zandt. I had only seen him on TV on the early Austin City Limits. I liked him and thought he was great, but I'd never seen him live, never met him, never gotten drunk with him. A woman I knew was friends with him, and she said, 'Do you want to go see Townes Van Zandt? He called me up, and I'm on the guest list.'"

Dave was free that night and accepted the invitation. It was the second show, and it was obvious to Dave by the way they came down the stairs that they felt no pain. Townes and Guy each navigated their way through their first song. "Then the woman I was with leans over to me and says, 'This one's going to be a white-knuckler.' And it was…but it had moments." They did manage to make it through the set list, and Dave had an opportunity to meet Townes after the show, which also proved memorable.

In an interview in the *Los Angeles Times*, Loudon Wainwright III also recalled seeing Guy and Townes at McCabe's, noting that it was really something to behold. In a place that served nothing stronger than black coffee, he went on to say that Townes and Guy were incredibly, gloriously plastered. In his view, this was a beautiful thing to behold. He recalled that it was like the audience too was tipsy, like a contact drunk, reflecting that McCabe's was a conduit in so many different ways.

Peter Case also remembered seeing the two Texans: "Townes and Guy together was great—the best I'd ever seen either of them. Maybe they inspired each other. A great night. Both were very awake, funny, moving, energetic." Perhaps he went to the early show.

Kirk Silsbee also got to see and meet his own music hero one memorable night at McCabe's: "I loved Richie Havens. I loved the music, I loved the artist, I loved his attitude." Richie Havens's career blossomed during the 1960s in the clubs of Greenwich Village in New York City, and he was catapulted to international stardom as the first artist to perform at the Woodstock Music Festival in 1969, with his legendary medley of "Motherless Child" and "Freedom" documented on the festival's live album and feature film. Kirk had collected most of his albums while in high school, and he attributed the artist's music with being the driving force that helped him navigate through adolescence. So, it was with great anticipation that Kirk came to McCabe's, this time with his wife, to see the legendary vocalist, guitarist, composer, and song interpreter.

Kirk was sure to make his reservations in advance; however, when he arrived, he was a bit surprised to see all the seats were already occupied.

Wayne Griffith, who had started working on concert nights in the early 1970s, explained that before McCabe's issued actual tickets, they simply accepted reservations over the phone and often took a few more than the seating capacity would allow, as, typically, not everyone who had asked for a seat showed up on the night of the concert. There was also a period when, if you brought a plate of chocolate chip cookies, you could get in for free. Some nights, everyone did show up, and sometimes, there were a lot of cookies. This was one of those nights.

Undeterred, Kirk said to the person at the door, "I know you can't put us on the floor, but you have that little room upstairs that has the glass window that looks down over the stage. We'd be tickled to death to go up there." Up they went.

Meanwhile, photographer Gary Glade was upstairs with Richie to shoot a portrait for the McCabe's wall of fame. Gary recalled, "He was very gracious and kindly asked where I would like him to go." They first walked into the recording room where Kirk and his wife sat waiting for the show to begin. Kirk, who had walked in on John Fahey so many years before, was now being walked in on, but this time, he wasn't speechless.

Kirk recalled the moment: "In walks Havens. This is my guy right there, I nodded to him, and I said, 'Mr. Havens, I just have to tell you…you got me through high school,' and I meant it. He seemed to be gratified by that."

With the recording room occupied, Gary guided the musician into one of the adjacent practice rooms. The photographer recollected that "he [Havens] sat down with that Guild guitar and started playing and singing a beautiful song I had never heard while I shot. I was struck by the thought that this man opened the Woodstock Festival in 1969 playing to 500,000 people. At this moment, he is playing to me—just me. An extraordinary McCabe's moment."

On the other hand, the night guitarist Nels Cline got to meet one of his idols backstage at McCabe's, things did not go quite so well. Cline remembered it was a Richard Thompson concert:

> *One evening after he played, I found myself backstage with a number of musical legends who had attended the show. Some had sat in with Richard. John Chelew noted me staring perhaps awkwardly/expectantly at one of my earliest musical heroes, Roger McGuinn. He walked up to me and cautioned, "Whatever you do, do not mention the Byrds."*
>
> *There was really bad blood between Byrds drummer Mike Clark, who was playing around the country as the Byrds, and other ex-members, and*

McGuinn was in what seemed to be a low point in his career. After this, I found myself face to face with McGuinn, and I couldn't resist telling him how very important his music was to me, which obviously led to the Byrds whether I mentioned the name or not. He gave me a cold stare, turned his back, walked away. But I didn't care. I said what I had to say. I was warned!

Chet Atkins, Shawn Colvin, Jesse Winchester, Nanci Griffith, Dan Hicks, Greg Brown, Iris Dement, John Sebastian, and U. Utah Phillips were just a few of the renowned artists from across the country who made McCabe's part of their touring itinerary. Counterculture artists like jazz poet Gil Scott-Heron and psychedelic philosopher Timothy Leary also found a home on the stage in the back room.

Then there was Wesley "Wes" Stace, who started his career performing as John Wesley Harding, a British musician who would go on to perform dozens of times at McCabe's. One of these appearances was particularly memorable for those on stage and in the audience.

Wesley recounts, "My story starts in England when I was reading about things happening at McCabe's, and it sounded like a really cool place to be." Wesley traveled to the United States in 1989 to record his first album in Los Angeles, and he wrote and recorded the song "Things Snowball" with Peter Case, who was playing at McCabe's one night. Peter invited Wesley on stage to perform the song, and thus began his long, loving relationship with the venue. Wesley's next appearance was also as a special guest, this time with singer/songwriter Steve Wynn and his band. He enjoyed this experience so much that he basically "stole" Steve's band for his first U.S. tour. The band included Robert Lloyd, a multi-instrumentalist who would go on to become a regular accompanist on Wesley's concert tours.

Robert, the music editor for the *LA Weekly* in the 1980s who went on to write for the *Los Angeles Times*, also played at McCabe's with Syd Straw and Victoria Williams. One day, on a whim, Robert bought a mandolin from the shop. He quickly learned to play and became the "guy with the mandolin," which led to a lot of work. Robert figured he's probably played at McCabe's as often as anyone in the world: "It became like a home, a very friendly place to play."

Signed to Sire Records, Wesley had been touring nationally in large venues as a support act for others on the label. However, he felt as though he should be playing folk clubs. He appealed to his agent: "'Will you please book me at this place McCabe's? That's where I really want to play.' And he did—and I walked out of there feeling like I was king of the world."

For his first show, Wesley shared a bill with Dave Alvin, Ronee Blakley, Elizabeth Barraclough, and the Paley Brothers. Now, he was really hooked, and he continued to play McCabe's every time he was on the West Coast.

He recalled one time, after his show was over, he was poking around the store when he found a copy of the hardcover edition of *The Beatles Complete Scores* that had a list price of nearly $100. Wes had wanted the book for a long time, so he decided to splurge. He asked the McCabe's staff to reduce his fee for the night accordingly. They told Wes he could have the book with their compliments. "It is such a nice and friendly place to do business," he said.

One night while he was in Los Angeles and not on his favorite stage, Wes attended a concert by the Rock Bottom Remainders at the Trocadero, and while he was standing in the back of the club, he found himself next to one of *his* musical heroes, Bruce Springsteen. At the time, Bruce was living in L.A. Never shy about striking up a conversation, Wes chatted to Bruce in back of the hall for forty-five minutes, and they exchanged email addresses.

A few months later, Wes was scheduled for a weekend at McCabe's, two shows on both Friday and Saturday, and he sent an invitation to Bruce to attend as his guest. Wes was not holding out much hope that his new friend would take him up on his offer, but just in case Bruce did arrive, Wes and Robert Lloyd (who now played with Wes on a regular basis) decided to work up the Bruce Springsteen song "Wreck on the Highway." Sure enough, Friday night came, and, in fact, a Springsteen did arrive—but it was the actress and photographer Pam Springsteen, Bruce's sister.

Then on Saturday, while preparing for the early show backstage, Wes looked up, and there was Bruce standing in the doorway: "He comes in, says, 'Hi, it was so nice to meet you the other day,' sits down. I introduce him to everybody. We have a beer." After they chatted a while, Wes said, "By the way, we happen to know one of your songs, 'Wreck on the Highway.' Do you want to do it with us?" Bruce agreed.

Wes is well known for his entertaining stage banter and keen sense of humor, so when he was called back for his encore at the early show and introduced his special guest, the audience rightly assumed it was a little joke. However, the chuckles soon turned to a collective, incredulous gasp and then to whoops and chants of "Bruuuuuce!" as the legendary rocker bounded down the stairs.

While they rehearsed together for only a short time backstage, the performance was flawless, with Bruce singing harmony and playing lead guitar.

Once again, photographer Gary Glade was there and was provided a surprise opportunity for him to meet his music hero:

> *After we had finished taking photos, I looked up, and Bruce was standing there by himself. I thought, "This is my chance to talk to Bruce." So, I said, "You know, about 1973, you came to Houston, unknown, and played four nights at Liberty Hall. I went down and was so knocked out by you, your songs, and your band that I went back the next night to see you again. About six months later, you came back to play four shows billed as 'The Lone Star Comes Back to Texas.' When we got to the Sportatorium (a funky roller derby place), the place is dark, all locked up with a small sign on the gate—'Bruce Springsteen show is cancelled due to lack of ticket sales.' We were bummed." At that point, Bruce stopped me and said, "Man, I want to shake your hand! I finally got to meet one of the ten people that bought tickets to that show!" And he shook my hand. My favorite rock and roll moment.*

Meanwhile, the stunned audience was slowly filing out of McCabe's, sharing their amazing experience with the line of fans queuing up for the late show who found it a little hard to believe that the "Boss" had actually performed as part of a John Wesley Harding concert. Any doubts turned to amazement as the parade of concert attendees from the first show was followed by Bruce himself headed out of McCabe's. The thrill of seeing the legendary musician pass by was quickly replaced by disappointment, as they realized that Bruce was leaving and would not be appearing on stage in the late show.

While having Bruce Springsteen as a special guest in the 150-seat room is certainly a standout, it is just one of many highlights for Wesley Stace: "It's a great, great place. I love going there with the sure knowledge that if I'd lost a capo or a pick…I could buy one…or if I needed a second guitar that I would be handed one."

John Chelew also managed to orchestrate the return of Arlo Guthrie, now a folk music icon, twenty-seven years after he showed up as a special guest in the second impromptu concert by Ramblin' Jack Elliott in 1969.

Arlo recalled:

> *Prior to the 1996 gig at McCabe's, I was a visitor from time to time, just waltzing around the shop with friends who shared interests in good guitars. My visits to the left coast were not very frequent. I usually showed up in the area about twice a year, mostly for gigs or recording. In the mid '90s, we were driving everywhere in a tour bus with a full band and crew, so we didn't*

linger. During the '60s to mid-'70s, we flew everywhere, usually with my girlfriend, Caroly, or the girl I met at the Troubadour and married, Jackie.

There was a shift from traditional-style folk music, which was really popular for a brief time, to the music evolution that included electric instruments. There were plenty of places that could accommodate them all, but McCabe's remained an acoustic venue (for the most part) for a long time. For what I was paid for a three-night stand at McCabe's was roughly about the same as what I would have got for a one-night stand anywhere else. The idea was to help out McCabe's (don't know if it did or not). Before then, it wasn't financially feasible to perform in such an intimate room, even though it had a great audience. Unlike anywhere else though, you could see what people were doing as their hands played the instruments. There's something great about a small venue. You could learn something, see something, and go home and try it yourself. Educational entertainment. The audience at McCabe's was knowledgeable and really fun. They appreciated the folk music traditions, and although I wasn't a traditionalist, I was warmly received.

In an interview with the *Los Angeles Times*, John Chelew recalled that a friend of Arlo was in the audience for the final night of his three shows: "Arlo was getting ready to go on stage and Allen Ginsberg was there because we had him booked the next night, and [he] asked if he could talk to Arlo, as he hadn't seen him in twenty years. The two got together and had a lengthy discussion." John recounted that sometime later, when Arlo was playing the new Ash Grove on the Santa Monica Pier, he started fingerpicking one of those "motorcycle blues" kinds of storytelling songs, and he started talking about seeing Ginsberg after twenty years at McCabe's.

That same year, the Fairfield Four, an a cappella gospel group was booked at McCabe's, and John Fogerty of Creedence Clearwater Revival fame, who was in town recording his album *Blue Moon Swamp*, came to the show. When he arrived, he asked if he could talk to the group, and was led into a room where photographer Gary Glade was shooting portraits of the group. Gary recounted that John Fogerty actually invited the group to join him in the studio the next day, where they accompanied him on one of the songs on the new record, "Hundred and Ten in the Shade." Gary made sure to capture the moment on film.

John Chelew concluded the interview with the *Times* reflecting that McCabe's was such a great meeting place for so many different people, where people could renew connections they may have lost. He said music has a way of reminding us of who we are and who we can be.

PHOTO GALLERY

Gary Glade

Gary Glade recalls becoming one of McCabe's photographers:

> *My photo relationship with McCabe's Guitar Shop began in 1990, when I went there to see Joe Ely, a dynamic, energetic performer. I sat up close with my camera, made some eight-by-tens and gave them to John Chelew. He was knocked out and said, "Man, these are great! Any time you want to come down and shoot another show, give me a call, and I'll put you plus one on the guest list."*
>
> *Well, for a photographer who loves music—always trying to sneak a camera into concerts—getting the blessing, free admission with a front row seat, and access to the performers at a venue booking some of the top people in folk, country, blues, and acoustic rock, this was music to my ears. McCabe's is different than shooting a show at a bar or a concert; it is more like shooting in church, where the audience has a great reverence for the music. Some acoustic performers are so quiet that even the click of the camera shutter is an intrusion, and a blinding flash is out of the question.*
>
> *One of my favorite things was the grace with which McCabe's allowed me to be present in the upstairs/backstage area where the performers hang, to interact with them or just listen and absorb as a fly on the wall. I loved the conversations and the impromptu music sessions that would just happen when musicians get together, sometimes unlikely and unexpected music. McCabe's Guitar Shop was an important touchstone in my life. My home away from home. Family.*

The following photos were taken by Gary Glade.

Left to right: John Wesley Harding, Bruce Springsteen, and Robert Lloyd.

Arlo Guthrie.

The Fairfield Four with John Fogerty.

Left to right: Townes Van Zandt, Kinky Friedman, and Guy Clark.

Peter Case.

Ramblin' Jack Elliott (*left*) and U. Utah Phillips (*right*).

George Thorogood (*left*) and John Hammond (*right*).

Chet Atkins.

Gillian Welch.

This page, top: John Chelew (*left*) with Jimmie Dale Gilmore (*right*) in the store after hours.

This page, bottom: Richie Havens.

Opposite: Edgar Meyer (*left, in the background*) and T Bone Burnett (*right*).

Leo Kottke.

Mark O'Connor.

Above: Ralph Stanley (*left*) and Curley Ray (*right*).

Left: Justin Townes Earle.

Tom Paxton.

CJ Chenier.

Odetta.

22
BRING THE FAMILY

Take One

Gerry McCabe and his first wife, Marcia Berman, separated soon after the guitar shop opened. However, Marcia remained in Los Angeles, and her notoriety as a children's music entertainer and recording artist soon helped inspire a series of family concerts that started in January 1970, soon after McCabe's started presenting performances at the store.

Collaborating with a diverse group of musicians throughout her career, Marcia recorded eleven albums, incorporating multicultural influences and fostering a positive self-identity and sense of empowerment in children by introducing songs about expressing feelings, friendship, cooperation, and a respect for the environment. John Wood, who, along with his partner Pam Wood, would go on to produce the children's concert series, met Marcia in the early 1970s.

In an article in the *Topanga New Times*, John recalled that when Marcia sang "the world stopped turning for a brief moment," and he and Pam became immediate fans. Pam noted that she was appreciative of Marcia's willingness to try new things, like choreography or different harmonies. Through the family concerts, John and Pam, who performed under the name J.P. Nightingale, helped grow an audience base of supportive families and engaged other children's music entertainers, including Dan Crow, to perform at the Sunday morning concerts.

Dan moved to Los Angeles in 1976 and soon heard about the children's concerts at McCabe's. Dan remembered:

> *I contacted John Wood about auditioning for the series. I was nervously excited, since this was the only venue that was doing this in L.A. at the time other than the Bob Baker Marionette Theater. John, Pam, and Marcia came to see me perform in a classroom of first graders, and thank goodness, they liked what I did and they hired me to do a concert at McCabe's. As I recall, we had nearly a full house. That was the beginning of over thirty years of my connection with McCabe's and my lifelong friendship with Fred, John, Pam, Marcia, Uncle Ruthie of* [public radio station] *KPFK fame, Patty Zeitlin, and Peter Alsop.*

When Marcia, John, and Pam stopped producing the series, Myrna Palma took their place and kept Dan in the rotation. In 1987, Dan started recording for the recently created Rounder Kids label, including the album *Chanukah at Home*, which featured Marcia, John, Pam, Fred Sokolow and Uncle Ruthie. There was an album release party at McCabe's, and the show toured for the next fifteen years. "I have to hand it to McCabe's for being such visionaries in regard to successfully running the Children's Concert Series," said Dan.

While folk singer Peter Alsop played his first shows at McCabe's in the 1980s as part of the evening concert series, it wasn't long before he transitioned to performing the kids' matinees. He found that he could combine his doctorate in educational psychology and songwriting skills to demonstrate how teachers and human service professionals could help families discuss sensitive issues, such as child abuse, loss and grief, and chemical dependency. He soon became a regular feature at education conferences across the country, and he used the model to fashion a family show that he performed on numerous occasions at McCabe's. He also created a summer family concert series at the Will Geer Theatricum Botanicum in nearby Topanga Canyon to complement the McCabe's kids concerts that took place during the rest of the year.

Marcia Berman. *Photo provided by Hally McCabe.*

As the new millennium dawned, a new crop of artists playing kids music arrived on the scene. They realized that their performances were a lot more successful if their attendees had the chance to move around. Justin Roberts played McCabe's on a number of occasions with his band the Not Ready for Naptime Players: "I remember that they would always take down the guitars before the kids shows. I guess those shows were more punk rock than the evening shows with the kiddie mosh pits and everything."

Although the dance party atmosphere—also offered in the back room by Dan Zanes, Ralph's World, and They Might Be Giants—was common, Justin noted that "playing at McCabe's feels like playing in your own living room. I remember one time, I asked the kids if anyone was ever afraid of the dark right before playing the song 'Thought It Was a Monster,' and this young girl stood up and started telling this eloquent story about a magic pillow her mother had given her. And when she finished, the whole crowd broke into applause. The room fostered that kind of communal experience. A pretty magical place."

Santa Monica native Kora "Koko" Peterson spent a lot of time at McCabe's Guitar Shop. Her mother, Vicki Hill, started working and teaching guitar there in 1993, and her sister, opera singer Jessica Sandidge, now gives voice lessons at the shop. "I grew up at McCabe's. It's very much been a part of my life," Koko stated. She started working at the store on the retail floor while she was in high school, and she soon became a member of the concert staff. Even when she left to go to college, she returned to work on holidays.

In 2016, Koko returned to Santa Monica and resumed working concerts. Then she was asked to start producing the family concerts: "I had never done anything like that. But they said, 'You have a kid—you do the kids shows.' I did have a kid, but she never listened to kid's music. She was listening to Taylor Swift. I was very nervous about it but always appreciated a challenge, so I dived into it like a research project."

Koko particularly recalled the multimedia performances by Gustafer Yellowgold as a highlight of her years producing the family concerts. Her experience led to her become McCabe's director for the evening concerts as well, starting in 2018.

Koko's family is just one of many who have called McCabe's their home away from home. The shop has always been supportive of its employees who sometimes need to have their children with them—well before "Bring Your Child to Work Day" was created.

Gerry McCabe and Marcia Berman's daughter Hally worked and gave guitar lessons at the store. Ruth Barrett, a pioneering contributor to the California mountain dulcimer renaissance of the 1970s and '80s, taught the instrument at McCabe's for fifteen years and performed on its stage, opening shows for folk legends Malvina Reynolds, Jean Redpath, Bert Jansch, and Jean Ritchie. Her daughter Amanda, while growing up, spent a fair amount of time at the shop and went on to form the Ditty Bops, a ragtime-influenced indie folk duo who was signed to Warner Brothers Records and played the McCabe's stage numerous times between 2006 and 2011.

Music school director and guitar repairman John Zehnder's children were also often at the store. Twins Tim and Tom would assist with the inventory as kids, and the family all performed in public for the first time at the McCabe's holiday show. They now return to the stage each year for the occasion. John, who become an ordained Presbyterian minister, officiated the wedding of Nora Riskin and Walt McGraw, the current owners of McCabe's Guitar Shop.

Tom eventually started working the floor, and before long, he was managing Friday night shows and coordinating the shop's outdoor concerts. He subsequently became McCabe's first community liaison.

However, it was John Zehnder's daughter Laura who, at age thirteen, achieved the most notoriety in the family for her job at McCabe's—cleaning the restrooms. She famously left a note in the bathroom in the upstairs dressing rooms that is used by the artists. It was recounted on Mike Bloomfield's album *I'm With You Always*, recorded live at McCabe's. In the stand-alone second track, "Men's Room," Mike gave a shout-out to Laura by name and read the note aloud to the audience.

Her note read as follows: "Please try to aim a little better. I know and understand that the pocket of the urinal is a small target, but try a little harder please—standing directly over it if necessary—as it lets off a frightful odor for those who clean the floor. And do try to use the ashtray, as they were made specifically for that use. Floors were not—they were constructed for walking on."

23

BRING THE FAMILY

Take Two

While John Chelew proved to be a masterful concert director, his vision extended beyond the music that was being performed live on stage.

Mary Katherine Aldin reflected: "John had incredible producer chops. He would hear music and immediately be dividing tracks on the board. He had a very analytical approach, and it made him a really excellent producer. He could hear something raw on stage and would immediately have the album produced in his head. When John liked something, he was 'over the moon' enthusiastic about it."

John produced his first recording for Bert Jansch in 1980, enlisting musicians Albert Lee and Jennifer Warnes on the album. Records by Pentangle, the John Renbourn Group, and the Saccharine Trust followed.

Then in 1987, when John Hiatt was playing McCabe's, John Chelew had an idea for his next project.

Since first playing McCabe's, John Hiatt had left California for Nashville, but he continued to play the venue on his West Coast tours. John Hiatt said, "Around 1986, I'd gone out to play McCabe's and visit with my A&R guy at Geffen Records, who called me out to talk about the next record. I was sitting in his office, and he got a call from the president of Geffen…and he called us up to his office and sat us both down and informed us of something we didn't know, which was that I had been dropped the day before. So, I was no longer employed by Geffen."

John played his show at McCabe's and returned home to Nashville. He told his wife, "Well, I'm back in the van. Pack me a lunch. I gotta hit the road. I don't have a label. I got nothing."

It wasn't long before things started to look up again. "I got a call from Andrew Lauder, who ran Demon Records, which was Elvis Costello and Nick Lowe's label at the time," John said. "He had offered a budget to make a record. I told Andrew that my confidence was so shot, I didn't even know what kind of record I would make. And Mr. Lauder said, 'You could sing in the shower, and we'd put it out.' So, that was all I needed to hear."

Andrew Lauder's words brought back John's confidence. "A little encouragement goes a long friggin' way," John said.

John Hiatt shared the news with John Chelew the next time he played McCabe's, and he recalled the conversation went like this:

Chelew: "Who would you want to play on the record if you had your pick?"

Hiatt: "Well, Ry Cooder would be great, because I had played on his record and did two tours with him back in the late '70s and was a huge fan. Jim Keltner would be great on drums."

Chelew: "What if I could get those two guys?"

Hiatt: "Chelew…come on, man. They're not gonna do it.…These guys have played with…George Harrison."

John Hiatt played his show, road testing the new compositions that he was working on. John Chelew was knocked out hearing the songs and knew they were ready to be recorded. John Hiatt knew this as well: "That's been my MO since I started. As Guy Clark used to say when they asked him how he knew it was time to make a new record, he said, 'When I got ten good songs.'"

When John returned for his next shows at McCabe's, John Chelew had news for him: "Guess what? I talked with Cooder and I talked with Keltner, and they're up for it." Hiatt was incredulous, but Chelew assured him he was not kidding and added that they would need a bass player. "Who would you want?"

They were on a roll, so John's response was "Nick Lowe!" In fact, Hiatt had recorded some with Nick and had struck up a friendship with him. When the bassist was asked if he would like to participate, he readily agreed and booked a flight from Britain to Los Angeles.

"Next thing I knew, we had four days booked at Ocean Way Studios," John said.

With John Chelew acting as producer, the quartet navigated a tight schedule and walked out with the new John Hiatt record: *Bring the Family*. "The four of us just shared this common thrill....Everyone was delighted that it was so off-the-cuff and came out as well as it did," said John.

The album proved to be a major breakthrough, producing John's first ever charting single, "Thank You Girl," and other classics such as "Memphis in the Meantime," "Have a Little Faith in Me," and "Thing Called Love," which was covered by Bonnie Raitt on her blockbuster album *Nick of Time* and brought to the fore the long-deserved recognition that John Hiatt was one of America's finest songwriters.

As the success of *Bring the Family* and John's subsequent recordings brought him to venues with substantially more seats, he still recalls McCabe's fondly: "It's definitely a classic West Coast listening room—which very few exist—and of course, it has the cool factor of doubling as a guitar shop."

On John Hiatt's legacy at McCabe's, music journalist Steve Baltin reflected, "John Hiatt, to me, represents McCabe's. I always remember him saying there's no other place in the world that has lamps like these....He played some incredible shows there."

24
ROCK 'N' ROOTS

As John Chelew found the demand for his skill as a record producer increasing, he ultimately decided to concentrate on that side of the music business and left McCabe's. He eventually worked on albums by Richard Thompson, Los Lobos, Peter Rowan, the Blind Boys of Alabama, Martin Carthy, and Ruthie Foster, among others.

Booking next fell into the hands of Zachariah "Zach" Love.

Born and raised in Los Angeles, Zach played guitar in a number of punk, pop, and rock bands around the city, and the first show he happened to see at McCabe's was that epic pairing of Charlie Haden with the Minutemen. He continued to attend the eclectic rock and jazz offerings at McCabe's, where he struck up a friendship with John Chelew. In 1990, Zach became a member of the concert staff, "tearing tickets, taking out trash" for a couple of years. He eventually became John's assistant, and after a while, he started working in the shop during the day as well, pursuing his interest in computers and internet technology.

With encouragement from store owner Bob Riskin, who was noted for being ahead of the curve when it came to computers, Zach helped to usher McCabe's into the digital age, building its website and eventually setting up online ticket sales.

As concert director, Zach continued to build on the eclectic scope of McCabe's bookings, with a special focus on rock, world music, and jazz, while never abandoning the shop's folk and Americana roots. Zach proudly recalled outstanding performances by Steve Lacy, Roswell Rudd Quartet, Fountains of Wayne, the Freedy Johnston Band, and the Throat Singers of Tuva.

Zach found solid audience support for all these genres and rarely heard gripes about the bookings or the sound level at the louder concerts. "When we would have something like Buckethead playing at McCabe's, the people who might complain about volume were not at that show," he said.

In fact, the volume needle had spent some time on the far right of the dial on a number of earlier occasions. Bob and Espie Riskin's daughter Nora recalled walking into McCabe's one evening in the mid-1980s when this was the case. She was surprised to see that it was the band Spinal Tap (from the hit mockumentary film *This Is Spinal Tap*) in full costume rocking the building. She stayed for the whole show. It was loud.

While most bands who typically played rock clubs were still able to connect with audiences in the relatively sedate environs of McCabe's back room, not all were as successful as Zach would have liked.

For example, after finally securing and clearing the seats for a standing-room concert by one of his favorite bands, NRBQ, for a weekend of shows in 1998, he was quite disappointed: "NRBQ is used to playing in a raucous environment, with a bar and people that are well lubricated, and it didn't quite work at McCabe's."

One of Zach's bandmates in his group the Love Supremes was Lincoln Myerson, who was pursuing a career as a rock 'n' roll guitarist and bass player, and the two became close friends. When Lincoln found himself at a life and career crossroads with the convergence of a business he started going under and the end of a long-term relationship, Zach suggested he help out at McCabe's. Soon, Lincoln was feeling better about things, setting up for concerts and selling coffee. "My best buddy was there, and I loved music," Lincoln said.

Initially, Lincoln had also gotten to know about McCabe's through John Chelew as a teenager in the early '80s, when he was working at Rhino Records. John would often come in to hang out and talk music, and he subsequently invited Lincoln to attend shows at McCabe's.

As Zach started to refocus on the technology side of McCabe's, he gave an ever-increasing amount of responsibility to Lincoln. In 1999, an initiative to set up a concert streaming service was implemented by the Digital Club Network. The company planned to install cameras in select clubs around the country, including McCabe's, to bring live music to audiences on the internet. While this technology has since become sophisticated and widespread, particularly during the COVID pandemic shutdown of in-person live music venues, at the time, it was a cutting-edge concept.

When a symposium intended to launch the project and train the venue operators was scheduled to take place in New York City, Zach asked Lincoln if he could represent McCabe's at the event. Lincoln readily agreed, and it was here that he really learned to talk the talk and walk the walk of a concert presenter as he soaked up the conversations of the promoters from around the country who attended.

Two years later, when Zach decided to concentrate on the website and the onset of online ticket sales at McCabe's, he handed Lincoln the keys, and the fifth concert director felt fully equipped to hit the ground running. Lincoln sensed that he had finally answered his calling: "I'm just a huge music fan. My standard joke is that I got to meet all my heroes and I had to pay them, so they were nice to me!"

Lincoln continued to expand the scope of presentations at McCabe's, and while he fully understood the venue's historic significance as a showcase for the finest artists in Americana music, he was not overly concerned about what genres were performed on stage. Lincoln said, "David Bromberg once said something from the stage that has always resonated with me: 'Folk music is any music that you can sing along to even if you don't know the lyrics.'" Lincoln proceeded accordingly, engaging artists like Rhett Miller of the Old '97s, Patterson Hood and Mike Cooley of the Drive-By Truckers, and pianist Vienna Teng.

Then one night, when seeing one his favorite bar bands, Jackshit, a trio of top session musicians including Val McCallum (Jackson Browne's lead guitarist), bassist Davey Farragher, and drummer Pete Thomas (Elvis Costello's band's rhythm section), Lincoln decided he would take the "Crazy" Challenge, in which members of the audience were invited to sing the Willie Nelson classic backed up by the group. Favorably impressed with Lincolns's rendition, the band members joined him for a drink, and the conversation drifted to the possibility of Jackshit playing McCabe's. Although they typically played bars and clubs around the city, the band agreed to perform at the listening room, and after a tremendously successful premiere, they have since become a McCabe's institution, selling out every time they play the back room.

25

GUITAR TOWN

Just as many legendary guitarists have graced the McCabe's stage over the years, some of the guitars purchased at the shop have attained legendary status.

Likely the most famous of these guitars is that of Clarence White, a child prodigy who spent a fair amount of time at McCabe's Guitar Shop. As one of the pioneers of bluegrass flat-picking, Clarence was also one of the most in-demand session players in the 1970s, recording with Arlo Guthrie, Joe Cocker, Linda Ronstadt, Jackson Browne, and many others. He was a member of the Byrds from 1969 to 1973 and famously invented the electric guitar string bender (also known as the B-Bender) that had the effect of mimicking a pedal steel guitar.

In an interview for *Premier Guitar* magazine, Roland White, Clarence's brother and fellow bandmate in the Three Country Boys, who eventually became the Kentucky Colonels, explained how Clarence's iconic Martin D-28 was discovered at McCabe's. He recalled scouring Los Angeles pawnshops and music stores every month with the other members of the Kentucky Colonels, including Eric White Jr. and Billy Ray Lathum, in search of guitars. It was on one of these missions that they saw a 1935 Herringbone D-28 tucked away in a corner of McCabe's. The instrument had a mismatched, oversized fingerboard that was taped to the neck and an enlarged sound hole. Roland asked the person working the floor what they would take for the instrument "as is." He was quoted twenty-five or thirty-five dollars. The band scraped together the money and bought the guitar for Clarence. The guitar was repaired, and Clarence started performing and recording with it. He also played the guitar in an appearance on the nationally televised *Andy Griffith Show*. The guitar apparently had nine lives, as Clarence inexplicably shot at it with a pellet gun, used it as an ashtray, once filled it with wet sand, and accidentally drove over it with his band's van, according to an article in *Fretboard Journal*.

In 1960, nine-year-old Tony Rice, who was also in a family bluegrass band, encountered Clarence playing the D-28 and was offered a chance to try it out. The guitar would prove to be in Tony's future.

In 1965, Clarence put the D-28 up as collateral on a loan and never got it back. Tragically, in 1973, the master guitarist's life was cut short when he was struck by a car while loading equipment after a gig.

Two years later, Tony Rice found out the guitar was in the possession of the man who had taken it as Clarence White's collateral, so he tracked it down and bought it for $550. Affectionately named the "Antique," the guitar miraculously survived a tropical storm in 1993, when it spent hours submerged in floodwaters after Tony had to abandon his Florida home.

Tony played the guitar on various occasions throughout his career, including at his final public appearance in 2013 at his induction into the Bluegrass Music Hall of Fame. During this performance, he played the Antique on the song "Old Train," accompanied by Wyatt Rice, Ricky Skaggs, Jerry Douglas, Sam Bush, and Todd Phillips.

More recently, the Antique was found in the hands of guitar whiz Billy Strings, who, in 2023, performed three tunes on it to an audience of nearly fifteen thousand fans in Winston Salem, North Carolina.

Rick Ruskin, the Takoma recording artist who frequented the McCabe's stage quite often in the '70s, recalled buying his first electric guitar, a '50s-era Fender Duo-Sonic, at the shop: "It was the only electric they had, and it was hidden in the back with other used stuff. Bob Riskin wanted it gone and sold it to me for seventy-five dollars and threw in a Rickenbacker hard case." Rick also bought a new Koa OO-25K-2 Martin at the shop. In addition to performing and shopping at McCabe's, Rick gave music classes at the store. His students included Kristina Olsen, who went on to have a career as a singer/songwriter and guitarist in her own right, as well as Don Musser.

In addition to playing guitar, Don Musser also started building them, and his reputation as a skilled luthier was enhanced when his first two instruments landed at McCabe's Guitar Shop.

Tom Rush, who helped shape the folk revival in the '60s and usher in the singer/songwriter movement in the '70s, first played McCabe's in 1976, and when he returned the following year, he was searching for a new guitar. Tom recalled, "I needed a guitar—and I played dozens of them—and this one by Don Musser was clearly head and shoulders above the rest. Then I said, well, 'Who's this guy Don Musser?' I was told that he came here a year ago and bought this book *How to Build a Steel String Guitar* and this is the second guitar he sold."

McCabe's had the first of these guitars, but it was in the shop being customized for the left-handed guitarist who had purchased it earlier, Peter Fonda. Best known as an actor for his role in *Easy Rider* and other films, Peter was also a musician and in fact released a single in 1967, the Gram Parsons–penned "November Night."

Since there were only two Musser guitars in circulation at the time, Tom settled on number two: "I paid $750 for it—I got the artist's discount." The Musser became Tom's go-to instrument and is well seasoned. Decades later, in 2023, Musser guitar number one resurfaced. "I found that Don Musser guitar signed by Peter Fonda on eBay, and I bought it," he said.

Don Musser guitars would go on to become highly prized instruments, also seen in the hands of Tom Petty, Bob Dylan, and Neil Young.

Fran Banish, a blues and rock guitarist who spent many years as an instructor at McCabe's, recalled an instrument that was brought back to life by McCabe's expert repair service: "Tommy Chong—from [comedy duo] *Cheech and Chong*—had a black 1939 Gibson L00 that he left in the trunk of his car, and the bridge pulled off of it along with some wood. He brought it into McCabe's to get fixed." The staff assessed the damage and advised him that it would be a multistep process to repair—it could possibly be in the shop for a few months. So instead, he traded in the guitar and bought another from the shop. Once the damaged guitar was fixed, Fran bought it.

Originally from Baltimore, bass player Marty Rifkin saved his money to travel to California; he eventually bought a van and arrived in 1978. His first stop was McCabe's Guitar Shop, where he bought a Dobro, although he had never played one. He lived the California "dream" (living in his van)—for a while anyway—before traveling to New York City and then back to Maryland, where he took lessons from Dobro legend Mike Auldridge of the bluegrass band the Seldom Scene.

Marty returned to Santa Monica in 1980 and, now proficient on the instrument, got a job teaching Dobro at McCabe's. Soon, Marty translated his Dobro skills to the pedal steel guitar, and before long, he found himself in high demand as a sideman for a number of groups in Los Angeles

Tom Rush with the first two Don Musser guitars. *Photo provided by Tom Rush.*

on weekends while working on the floor and teaching lessons upstairs at McCabe's during the week.

Thanks to the support and flexibility of the McCabe's management, Marty was able to keep his commitments as a sideman and in-demand session player with the likes of Bruce Springsteen, Tom Petty, Glen Campbell, Buddy Miller, Dwight Yoakum, and "Weird Al" Yankovic. In 2013, McCabe's staged a memorial tribute to JJ Cale, who had played McCabe's in 1981 and again in 2009, where he was joined by special guests Mike Campbell and Tom Petty. The band for the tribute concert included Eric Clapton, Jim Keltner, and Don White, as well as Marty Rifkin on bass, performing covers of Cale's songs, including "After Midnight" and "Cocaine."

In addition to that first Dobro, Marty bought several other instruments at McCabe's, but one really stands out in his memory. One day, while he was working the floor, a woman brought in a 1954 double-neck eight-string Fender steel guitar, explaining that her husband, the instrument's owner, had passed away and she wanted to sell it to the store. Although Marty was exclusively playing the pedal steel at that point, he fell in love with the instrument. In typical McCabe's fashion, eschewing any profit, they encouraged Marty to purchase the instrument directly from its owner.

Marty bought the guitar with the intention of keeping it more as a collector's item than an instrument he would play in concerts or recordings, but two days later, he sprained his ankle and was therefore unable to operate the pedals on his regular instrument. So, he brought his recently acquired instrument to his next gig. And for the next eighteen years, it was the only steel guitar he played live in concert.

Multi-instrumentalist David Lindley was a regular at McCabe's, both on stage and at the sales counter. Raised near Pasadena, east of Los Angeles, David grew up listening to his father's eclectic record collection. Before long, he picked up a ukulele and then the banjo. As a teenager, he won the Topanga Canyon Banjo Contest five times (including playing the five-string with a violin bow), and he formed the Mad Mountain Ramblers and the Dry City Scat Band, which played around the Los Angeles folk clubs and at Disneyland. It wasn't long before David started playing guitar and violin, and in 1966, he formed the psychedelic band Kaleidoscope, which recorded four acclaimed albums through 1970.

Subsequently, David went to England to work with Terry Reid and then came back to the United States, where he toured and recorded extensively with Ry Cooder and Jackson Browne. He may be best remembered for his soaring lap steel slide guitar solo on "Running on Empty," the title track and hit single from Jackson's 1977 live album. (And that's David singing the falsetto on the album's closing track "Stay.")

David soon found that his instrumental virtuosity was in high demand, and before long, he was appearing on albums by Bob Dylan, James Taylor, Iggy Pop, Linda Ronstadt, Dolly Parton, John Prine, David Crosby, Graham Nash, Ben Harper, Rickie Lee Jones, and Bruce Springsteen.

David started recording albums with his own band El Rayo-X in the 1980s and performed at McCabe's numerous times solo. He also appeared with Terry Reid, percussionists Wally Ingram and Hani Naser, and with other musicians. McCabe's made sure that David was on stage in the all-star shows celebrating Nancy Covey's retirement and the shop's fiftieth anniversary. David's interest and ability to master any instrument with strings—mandolin, dobro, hardingfele, bouzouki, cittern, bağlama, gumbus, charango, cümbüş, oud, and zither—and his passion for collecting them (it has been said he owned more than one hundred), made him a regular customer at his hometown store, the Claremont Folk Music Center, as well as at McCabe's.

Bob and Espie Riskin recalled that David's enthusiasm for accumulating stringed instruments was brought to their attention one day when they received a phone call at the shop: "His wife told us not to sell him anymore instruments."

For Larry Campbell, it was the guitar he did not buy at McCabe's that stands out in his memory: "I almost bought one but talked myself out of it, and I'm still kicking myself in the ass for it. It was a vintage 00028 Martin. It would've been a lot of cash. I coulda done it. I shoulda done it. And [it] would be worth twice what I would have paid for it by now."

Arlo Guthrie never did buy a guitar from McCabe's but recalled, "I loved going to McCabe's, as they were one of the only guitar shops in the early days that had really decent guitars, like Martins, Gibsons, Guilds, etc. We'd play 'em all just to know who was making good stuff. Loved the smell of the wood."

Peter Rowan agreed, "Of course, at McCabe's, I always check out the instruments. There are some really choice guitars hanging on the wall! I always give them a strum! And the luthiers of the repair shop have helped me countless times to keep my axe in good shape!"

Peter Case has probably spent more time than any other performer on McCabe's stage and in the store: "I play the guitars they get in, all those great Collings…and the Gibsons, and Martins, etc. that find their way through. I bought a Taylor there once, also an imported Indian harmonium, which I've used a lot in recording. Tons of harmonicas, capos, strings, and thumb picks.... They used to special order the strings I used. No one else carried them."

Richard Thompson was also somewhat of a regular customer: "I would always check out the guitars! Not sure I ever bought one, but I bought a harmonium, various drums and percussion, dulcimers, amps, and lots of music books from their well-stocked shelves."

In an article for *Fretboard Journal*, guitarist Adam Levy wrote about going to see the Cajun band BeauSoleil at McCabe's. As would often happen when Richard was in town, BeauSoleil invited him up to play on the last two songs of their set. As he approached the stage, a McCabe's staffer grabbed a Fender Stratocaster "Squier" off the wall—the beginner's model of the legendary guitar maker's line—and offered it to Richard with the tags still on. Adam recalled that from Richard's first note, it was clear that this guitar was putty in his hands. He noted that it was a rare gift for any guitarist to be able to play with such ease on an unfamiliar instrument.

In an interview with Richard, Levy stated he was curious to know how he managed to sound so great on a $250 guitar he'd never touched before. Richard confessed that he was a bit intimidated by people who can pick up any guitar and sound great, but he remembered what Norman Blake once said: "that a bad guitar can only do one thing, but he will search for that thing on that guitar until it sounds good." He admitted it is always preferable to perform on your own gear, but at McCabe's, you can just pull something off the wall and hope it has a gauge of string that you can work with. Richard confessed that although it was bit random, it was actually a lot more fun.

Just as famous folks appeared on McCabe's stage, familiar faces occasionally turned up to see what was for sale at the shop. Actor Robert Downey Jr. came into the store with his assistant and systematically cleaned the store out of every African drum they had because his kids wanted to learn percussion.

Guitar repairman Ron Chambliss remembers George Harrison coming in and purchasing a National steel ukulele, all the while sharing his enthusiasm for a reissue of Hoagy Carmichael's recordings. Ron was slightly taken aback by the encounter with the former Beatle. No sooner did he manage to get back to work when he was summoned to the phone. It was George calling to give him the catalog number of the Carmichael CD so he could order it.

While Bob Riskin typically spent most of his time in his office, Espie Riskin recalled one day when he happened to be working on the floor: "Bob's in the store and this lovely young woman and her mother come in, and they were looking for a dulcimer. So, Bob goes into the whole history of the dulcimer… and the staff is going nuts." Bob was unaware of the staff's reaction as he regaled the two about the advantages of the dulcimer. The young woman ultimately decided to buy the instrument. Bob continued, "I asked her for her name and address for the warranty. And she said, 'I can't give that to you.'" Bob was puzzled, and meanwhile, the staff is cracking up, jumping up and down trying to point Bob in the direction of the song book prominently displayed on the counter. Finally, Bob saw the book, which featured a picture of the young lady about to purchase the dulcimer. It was Taylor Swift.

26

McCABE'S GOES GOLD(EN)

By 2008, Lincoln Myerson was firmly ensconced in his role as concert director, and when it was determined to stage a performance to celebrate the fiftieth anniversary of the opening McCabe's Guitar Shop, he was at the ready with a concept to laud the musical endeavors of the venerable establishment.

Lincoln's idea was to have his predecessors—Bobby Kimmel, Nancy Covey, John Chelew and Zach Love—as well as himself each program one part of the show to demonstrate how their unique visions combined to make the "Live at McCabe's Guitar Shop" series an eclectic, much-loved, and long-lasting institution.

It was mutually agreed on to hold the event at a nearby venue with a much larger seating capacity than the back room at McCabe's. The historic 1,800-seat Royce Hall at UCLA, about five miles northeast from the guitar shop, was reserved for the concert. (Ironically, this is the same hall that Elizabeth Cotten and Mike Seeger had been scheduled to play in 1969 before their show was cancelled. This led to them playing at McCabe's, giving birth to the concert series.) With big ideas and a minimal budget, artists were asked to perform gratis, with McCabe's covering travel expenses. So, it was necessary for the directors to reach out to their wish list of musicians directly, bypassing booking agents and artist managers as much as possible. Nancy Covey, who had remained in touch with the cadre of singers and songwriters she had engaged with during her decade of booking McCabe's through her Festival Tours enterprise, was quickly filling the schedule for the planned performance.

Lincoln came to realize that his original concept for each concert director to participate equally would therefore not materialize, and he set out on a mission to have another of his ideas come to fruition: engaging an unannounced surprise guest to appear as the cherry on top.

Chan Marshall, also known as Cat Power, who first performed at McCabe's in 1999 and returned as recently as 2006, was Lincoln's first choice. He thought her singular fusion of folk, punk, soul, and blues perfectly embodied the various genres for which McCabe's was well known, and Cat was at the top of her game, performing at prestigious theaters and festivals around the globe. Plus, he was personally acquainted with the singer, and she was living in Los Angeles at the time. He thought if he could make the ask directly, in person, she may very well consent. Lincoln's idea went well beyond just having Cat Power make an appearance at the concert. Odetta, the voice of the folk revival and civil rights movement who had appeared many times over the years at McCabe's, had already agreed to participate. One of her signature songs was "House of the Rising Sun," and likewise, Cat Power also included a compelling version of the classic in her repertoire. Lincoln thought it would be a touching, historic moment if Cat were to join the legendary singer to perform the song together, offering a multigenerational capstone to the golden anniversary concert.

Knowing that he had to make the pitch directly to Cat, he was pleased to see that she was scheduled to perform at the Hollywood Bowl on September 17, two weeks before the anniversary show. Lincoln decided to go to the concert to try to get an audience with Cat to share his idea. "Chan [Cat], at the time, was a chain smoker, and I knew that if I could get around to the stage door that I would run into her, because she would be outside having a smoke. Sure enough, just like clockwork, here comes Chan." The singer recognized Lincoln immediately and invited him backstage, where, after enjoying some wine, Lincoln shared his idea. Cat was thrilled. "Oh my God! Me and Odetta on the same stage? Are you kidding me? Of course, I'll do it!"

More than pleased with the outcome, Lincoln proceeded to call Odetta's manager and proudly shared his plan. However, the glow was quickly extinguished by her booking agent's response: "Odetta's not going to do that. She doesn't duet with people, and that's her closing number, and she's not going to share that number with anybody else.'"

A crestfallen Lincoln Myerson was not only disappointed, but now, he also had to find a way to uninvite Cat Power to participate in the concert as he envisioned. While screwing up his courage to dial her number, his phone rang—it was Cat Power. She was profusely apologizing and explaining that a gig had come up in Barcelona that she had to accept, but it would preclude her from participating in the McCabe's concert with Odetta. Secretly relieved to be off the hook, Lincoln assured Cat that he totally understood, and he thanked her for her consideration.

Moments later, his anxiety returned as Lincoln realized that he was now still without a surprise guest. Lincoln, who had been working closely with public radio station KCRW on publicizing the fiftieth anniversary concert, shared the situation with the program director of the station's music show *Morning Becomes Eclectic*, Ariana Morganstern, who, in turn, mentioned that Chrissie Hynde of the rock band the Pretenders was taping some songs for the show just a few days before the McCabe's concert. Perhaps she would agree to be the surprise guest.

Sure enough, Lincoln asked, she agreed, and days later, she sang some acoustic versions of Pretenders hits to a sold-out theatre.

It was a true McCabe's retrospective, with Richard Thompson leading a house band. The concert featured performances by Peter Case, Savoy Doucet Band, David Lindley, Rosanne Lindley, Bonnie "Prince" Billy, Peter Rowan, Ditty Bops, Dan Hicks, Blind Boys of Alabama, Kami Thompson, Los Lobos, Jennifer Warnes, and Jackson Browne. Loudon Wainwright III madly drove the one hundred miles to the theater after his gig in Santa Barbara and made it in time to join the party. Even Ricky Jay worked some magic into the evening. And yes, the seventy-eight-year-old folk music icon Odetta sang "House of the Rising Sun"—solo—causing Steven Mirkin to write in his review in *Variety* that it was hard for anyone to top the emotional impact of her quiet, steely dignity. The epic, five-hour show concluded with Van Dyke Parks dancing up the aisle with his accordion while everyone returned to the stage to sing "This Land Is Your Land."

PHOTO GALLERY

Greg Allen

Greg Allen has been active in the Los Angeles music scene for more than four decades as both a photographer and a graphic designer, and he is the cofounder of Omnivore Recordings. With an eye for detail and a vast knowledge of musical styles and eras, Greg has an eclectic design repertoire that encompasses classic album repackaging and new projects alike. He has designed box sets for Wilco, John Coltrane, Gram Parsons, Miles Davis, Ray Charles, and Alice Cooper as well as coffee-table books (*Creem: America's Only Rock & Roll Magazine*, *The Stooges: The Authorized & Illustrated Story*), soundtracks (*CBGB*, *Sex and the City*, *Hairspray*, and *A Christmas Story*), and catalog reissues for artists such as Elvis Costello, Fleetwood Mac, Yes, and the Stooges. Greg has served two terms on the board of governors for the Los Angeles chapter of the Recording Academy. Omnivore is grateful to whoever first gave this guy a camera. The following photos were taken by Greg Allen, www.omnivorerecordings.com.

Peter Case.

Rosanne Cash.

Left to right: Charlie Haden, Ginger Baker, and Shuggie Otis.

Beck.

Left: Bill Monroe (*left*) and Dwight Yoakum (*right*).

Below: Natalie Merchant of 10,000 Maniacs (*left*) and Michael Stipe of R.E.M. (*right*).

Opposite: Papa John Creach (*left*) and Jorma Kaukonen (*right*).

Gil Scott-Heron.

Zachary Love.

Lincoln Myerson (*left*) with Phranc (*right*).

John Hiatt.

Loudon Wainwright III.

Ali Farka Toure (*left*) and Ry Cooder (*right*).

Los Lobos at McCabe's fiftieth anniversary concert.

Richard Thompson at McCabe's fiftieth anniversary concert.

Jackson Browne at McCabe's fiftieth anniversary concert.

Odetta at McCabe's fiftieth anniversary concert.

27
THREE CHORDS AND THE TRUTH

You're still getting the basic G-C-D," says banjoist Patrick "Pat" Cloud with a grin after he plays a series of complicated chord fingerings up and down the neck of his five-string banjo in the documentary *Banjo Meltdown.*

Born in Los Angeles, Pat started his banjo odyssey strumming along to records by Earl Scruggs on an old Kay banjo. The instrument had three rusty strings, and his mother had previously used it as a wall decoration. He was eventually able to get a new set of five strings, and he taught himself to play by ear, slowing down his old Victrola record player from 33 RPM to 16 RPM. Although he knew there was no place for a banjo in his high school band, he still asked the music director if he could join. With a polite "no," the director instead supplied Pat with several music theory books, and he proceeded to teach himself how to read music.

Pat's horizons expanded when he went to the National Fiddle Contest in Weiser, Idaho. Pat recalled, "The biggest thing that turned me around was Oklahoma-Texas style fiddling. They had the greatest players there, and I was having a great time with these late-night jam sessions in this little town. And these guys would get together, and they'd take some fiddle tune like "Done Gone" and they would go chorus after chorus [and] take five- or ten-minute solos on the melodies of these tunes. And I said, 'Man, this is like jazz!'"

Chief among these fiddlers was Byron Berline, who had previously won the contest three times starting in 1965. Byron played with Bill Monroe and the Dillards, and went on to become a member of the Flying Burrito Brothers, Country Gazette, and a trio with banjoist John Hickman and guitarist Dan Crary. He moved to Southern California in 1969 (the same year he recorded his most famous tune as a session player, "Country Honk," with the Rolling Stones on their *Let It Bleed* album) and went on to play at McCabe's numerous times. Byron made a tape of fiddle tunes, which he gave to Pat, who, in turn, transcribed them for a five-string banjo.

Pat also attended Southern California's Topanga Banjo and Fiddle Contest and Folk Festival, and someone mentioned to him that McCabe's was looking for a banjo instructor. As a kid, Pat had frequented McCabe's Long Beach location, which was closer to his home. "I heard they had banjos," he said. There, he met fellow banjo picker John McEuen, but he was unfamiliar with the Santa Monica store. When he learned of the teaching opportunity, he thought, "That sounds like something I can do. So, I showed up and met Bob. He was a great guy, wonderfully eccentric and very smart."

The Bob was Bob Baxter, a popular teacher who authored several guitar instruction books and recorded the album *Fingerpickin' Blues* on Kicking Mule Records.

Bob offered Pat the job, provided that he could supply students with tablature to take home and practice. Pat could sight read standard music notation and could easily figure out how to play something by listening to records, but he had no success in trying to learn tablature. "I had the red Pete Seeger [*How to Play the 5-String Banjo*] book and couldn't make heads or tails of it."

Bob Baxter was not deterred. Pat recalled, "Bob drew a line on a piece of paper. He said, 'On the bottom of the line are the string numbers. For you, it would be one to five. And the top line is the fret number. That's the kind of tablature I use.' I said, 'Great! I could probably figure that out.'" He did, and he started giving banjo lessons.

Pat taught many students while at McCabe's, including Wayne Griffith, who would go on to become the venue's sound engineer and concert director, and John Schlocker, who would eventually succeed Pat as the shop's banjo teacher.

Pat recalled, "Then one day, Bob Baxter said, 'Look, there's this guy in Hollywood who would like you to make a house call. Would you be into that?'" Pat was unsure, but Bob insisted: "It'll be great. You'll have a lot of fun." Pat agreed, and indeed, it was more fun that he could have imagined. "So, I went there…nice guy with a dry sense of humor.…He had me laughing so hard, I could hardly play!" It was Jerry Stiller of the comedy duo Stiller and Meara who would one day become better known as Frank Costanza, the father of George on TV's sitcom *Seinfeld*.

Pat's musical curiosity ran deep and wide, and whenever he heard new music, he explored ways it could work on a banjo. However, his defining musical moment came soon after he started giving lessons. He attended a concert at McCabe's: "Joe Pass, sitting on the stage playing his guitar by himself. I said, '*Wow*—that is something.'" Pat bought the Joe Pass music instruction book at the shop and transposed the music for banjo. He subsequently started transcribing jazz saxophone solos from records. "If I couldn't play a sax phrase, I would just change a note or two here and there so I could retain the melodic integrity and make it more banjoistic," he said.

During his time at McCabe's, Pat was a regular on stage, playing everything from straight-ahead bluegrass to experimental jazz in a variety of configurations—solo, duos, and with the groups Amazing Phrasing and the Instant Brothers.

Pat Cloud left McCabe's when he was invited to join Keith Whitley and Jimmy Gaudreau in their bluegrass band New Tradition. He also recorded the jazz album *Higher Power* in 1983, wrote banjo instruction books, and now offers online lessons.

Longtime McCabe's music teacher Fred Sokolow was totally immersed in folk music in high school, and McCabe's was one of his favorite haunts: "I was into blues, old-time music and bluegrass. I was in the store a lot, and at one point—I was probably fifteen or sixteen—and I'm looking at this blues album by Eric Von Schmidt all up and down, and Walter Camp says, 'Would you like to take that home and borrow it for a while?' I did! I took it home for about a month and learned everything I could off it and brought it back."

While Fred left Los Angeles to go to college in Northern California, he never forgot the kindness he received at McCabe's. By the time he returned to Santa Monica in 1975, Fred had played with bluegrass luminaries like John Herald, Frank Wakefield, and Jerry Garcia; recorded two albums for

Pat Cloud's Jazz Band. *Photo provided by Pat Cloud.*

Kicking Mule Records; and begun touring with the Limelighters, Bobbie Gentry, and Jim Stafford.

He returned to Santa Monica in 1975 and went to McCabe's to see about the possibility of giving guitar lessons at the store, but John Zehnder indicated that, at that moment, they had all their bases covered. Instead, Fred went across town, where Bob Baxter, who had left McCabe's to open his own store called Guitar Workshop, offered him a teaching position. He remained there for the next several years.

When Bob Baxter closed up his shop in the mid-1980s and started working in the food industry (and later as an editor of *Skin & Ink Magazine*), Fred returned to McCabe's, where there was now room for his teaching skills.

His students have been many and include Bette Midler (as she prepped for the film *The Rose*), Glenn Campbell's daughter Ashley (who needed to learn to play banjo for her father's final tour), and Kristen Wiig (as she prepped for her role in *The Secret Life of Walter Mitty*).

Fred also performed on stage at McCabe's numerous times over the years, including in shows with Tom Paxton, joined by Theodore Bikel; Jody Stecher and Krishna Bhatt, who fused Indian classical music with country, Cajun, and folk; and Circle of Fourths, a group with fiddler Brantley Kearns that played bluegrass arrangements of rock songs. Fred was also a regular on stage at the children's concerts.

Dave Zeitlin was also a longtime presence at McCabe's, and he is fondly remembered as a guitar teacher who headed up the music and produced the advertising flyer—and as a gentle soul who contributed to McCabe's spirit like no other.

Kit Alderson has been giving both guitar and autoharp lessons ever since he returned to Santa Monica and became a member of McCabe's Floating House Band. His students have been many in his more than fifty years at the shop. They have most famously included Catherine O'Hara (for her role in the mockumentary *A Mighty Wind*) and Joaquin Phoenix and Reese Witherspoon (in preparation for their roles as Johnny Cash and June Carter, respectively, in *Walk the Line*). Kit's Hollywood students also included Tracey Ullman and Emily Rossum.

Both Fred Sokolow and Kit Alderson still teach at McCabe's as of this writing.

McCabe's proximity to Hollywood and the potential for doing movie soundtrack work were the impetuses for Chicago-born guitar slinger Fran Banish to relocate to Los Angeles in the late 1980s. He settled in West Los Angeles, where he was pleased to see that McCabe's was the closest guitar shop. Fran already knew all about the store from an article titled "McCabe's Guitar Shop: Supplementing Sales with Teaching and Performance" in the March 1977 issue of *Guitar Player* magazine. "I was completely enamored by the story of McCabe's," he said, "how various famous people came in and out of there and that Ry Cooder used to teach there.…I just thought, 'Wow, this is the coolest place—I gotta go there.'"

Fran would stop by McCabe's every few weeks to pick up strings and try out the guitars, playing the different styles in which he was fluent. He said, "I might pick up a classical guitar and play…Villa-Lobos or something—then I'd pick up a National steel, and I'd play blues.…I'd pick up a Martin and play some bluegrass riffs." Consequently, the folks at McCabe's got to know about the new guitar man in town. On occasion, Fran would ask, "Do you guys need another guitar teacher?" Only to hear that there were no openings.

Fran continued to play gigs around town while he worked for a temp agency and continued to make his presence known at McCabe's.

Finally, when the store's slide guitar teacher left for Nashville, John Zehnder invited Fran to bring in a résumé and syllabus for an eight-week class in slide guitar. "I ran home and typed it up and brought it back either the same day or the next morning," Fran said. He got the job and quit the temp agency. "It was actually a great moment in my life…a wonderful thing to get into McCabe's."

Fran taught the slide guitar class for a couple of years and also started playing the open mic sessions that were held each Sunday, organized by fellow teacher Gary Mandel. (Gary would eventually leave McCabe's and open his own store, Boulevard Music, that sells instruments, offers lessons, and presents concerts, about three and a half miles away.)

Once the slide guitar classes concluded, Fran began giving lessons to individuals who were interested in the blues, and he continued playing live shows in the area. He often went to Harvelle's, a historic club in downtown Santa Monica, to participate in the Wednesday night blues jam. It was there that he met Kevin Moore, better known as Keb' Mo' in the early 1990s.

Born and raised in Compton, California, Keb' spent the '70s and '80s playing with Papa John Creach and the Whodunit Blues Band. He was also a songwriter for A&M Records and had released a solo album.

Fran and Keb' enjoyed playing together, and they both got hired to accompany singer Louis Clemente, sharing electric guitar duties in a band that played the blues as well as Motown cover tunes. After playing a few gigs, they parted ways, but Keb' reached out to Fran when he landed the role of

Guitar Man in the George C. Wolfe play *Spunk*, based on the short stories of Zora Neale Hurston.

The role called for Keb' to play the blues on acoustic guitar. Fran recalled, "He knew I was teaching at McCabe's, so he came in and I gave him a crash course on fingerpicking blues. 'OK, you need to know alternating bass like Mississippi John Hurt, and you need to know monotonic bass like Lightnin' Hopkins, Mance Lipscomb, and getting into the Delta stuff.'" Next came a crash course on slide guitar. Keb' was a quick learner, and he went on to star in the play for three years.

Fran believes that the conversion from electric R&B to the acoustic country blues was the catalyst that caused Kevin Moore to walk out as Keb' Mo' once the tour concluded: "He started writing, and of course, Taj Mahal emerged as an inspiration for him."

In an interview in the *Harvard Review*, Keb' recalled that in 1969, his vocational drawing teacher got him into a concert that Taj Mahal was playing at his high school in Compton. Taj played two shows because the whole school couldn't fit into the auditorium all at once. And although the students were supposed to go to only one assembly, Keb' managed to go to both shows.

At the concert, Taj played a National steel resonator guitar, an instrument that Keb' had first laid his eyes on while waiting to get into a show at the Troubadour, where McCabe's had their satellite store. At the time, Keb' recalled wondering why there were guitars with hubcaps on them. Hearing the instrument in the hands of Taj Mahal, it all started making sense, and Keb' felt as if the universe was trying to point him to the blues.

Twenty-five years later, Keb's new persona, complete with National steel guitar, was documented on his self-titled album, which was released to great acclaim in 1994. And he followed it up with an extraordinary run of Grammy award–winning recordings.

When playing in Southern California, Keb' would occasionally invite Fran to sit in. And then in 2006, Fran played on Keb's album *Suitcase* and toured with the band on the West Coast and in Europe. Fran also collaborated in an instructional video with Keb' Mo' on Homespun Tapes and eventually gave some guitar lessons to Keb's son.

When Jackson Browne was invited to perform the "Grand Canyon Song" at a 1997 concert paying tribute to Steve Goodman, Fran was the man he sought to guide him in the bluesy picking pattern.

While Fran did not get the movie soundtrack work he had envisioned when he moved to the West Coast, he taught guitar to his share of Hollywood actors, including Ethan Hawke, Brad Pitt, John Lithgow, Will Ferrell, Julie Delpy, and Emile Hirsch. He also helped Christian Bale when he needed to channel Bob Dylan for his role in the film *I'm Not There*. Then there was Fran's most famous student—Bob Dylan himself.

> *Bob's middle son, Sam, and Jakob Dylan* [his youngest son] *used to come and hear the blues band I was playing with in the early '90s that also had Denny Croy on bass, who was a McCabe's stalwart. Denny was a bass teacher and also sales staff and manager. Sam started taking lessons from me....He was into acoustic blues. After a couple of years went on, Sam asked me if I would play at his wedding. That was a particularly fabulous experience. We were playing a mixture of blues rock and classic blues and we're at the Santa Monica Beach Club on this beautiful summer evening, and there in the middle of the dance floor is Bob Dylan dancing... in a tuxedo. That was a very surreal moment.*

A couple days later, when Fran was keeping his regular hours at McCabe's, yet another surreal moment occurred when he was informed that there was a call for him on line two. Fran recalls the conversation:

"Hi, it's Fran here."
"Hey. Fran. This is Bob."
"Bob? Bob who?"
"Bob Dylan from the other night. I saw you playing at Sam's wedding."

At first, Fran was convinced it was one of his friends pulling a prank, but he finally realized it was in fact Bob Dylan on the line.

Bob continued, "I really liked how you played...that Willie Brown tune 'Mississippi Blues.' That was like the best I ever heard. And I want to come in and take a lesson or two with you—go over something. I've been listening to Blind Lemon Jefferson a lot lately. Do you know 'Rabbit's Foot Blues?'"

Fran knew of the tune, as he had it on vinyl. He went home and woodshedded the tune, coming up with two transcriptions, one in standard tuning and one in open A tuning, so he could be prepared for the lesson.

Bob arrived at McCabe's and asked the folks at the counter, "Where's Fran?" The incredulous staff pointed upstairs to room number 3—a surreal moment for them. Fran recalled the lesson going well, with Bob learning the song really easily. While it was the only lesson Bob requested, Fran continued to teach Bob's sons Sam and Jakob on occasion.

After twenty-seven years in Los Angeles, Fran found that the interest in guitar was receding, and consequently, his number of lessons decreased. Simultaneously, the paying gigs for blues and rock bands were becoming harder to come by. After receiving an invitation from a cousin to return to Chicago to participate in his company that was producing commercials, Fran decided it may be best to return to his hometown and the rest of his family.

Not all of the music lessons at McCabe's were scheduled—some just happened by chance. Jack MacKenzie, a retail manager, repair technician, and aspiring guitarist who opened shows at McCabe's for Norman Blake, John McEuen, Joe & Rose Lee Maphis, Merle Travis, and Country Gazette, took only one guitar lesson in his life, but it was a memorable one:

> *Doc Watson was my idol. I heard him play in the early '70s and decided I wanted to play like that. I'm still trying to learn. I've only ever had one guitar lesson, and it was a brief one from Doc. I was picking along with him in the front room and played a bluegrassy lick. After the song, he said, "Son, you're working too hard," and showed me an abbreviated version of the same lick that was far easier than what I was doing and achieved the same sound. It kind of transformed my playing. That was my first and only guitar lesson. Good to quit when you are ahead, right?*

28

THE SWELL (AND NOT SO SWELL) SEASON

While Lincoln Myerson actively sought artists to fill the concert schedule, one of the most memorable shows during his tenure appeared almost by magic.

When Glen Hansard and Markéta Irglová, the duo known as the Swell Season, were in town to attend the 2008 Academy Awards (where they were nominated for Best Original Song for "Falling Slowly" from the movie *Once*), they stopped into McCabe's Guitar Shop.

Lincoln recalled, "They came into McCabe's, and I recognized them and introduced myself and showed them around." Lincoln walked them down McCabe's "Wall of Fame," a hallway crammed with photos of the many artists who have played the room over the decades. "Every artist that plays McCabe's—and I mean every artist—their favorite thing is wandering up and down the hallway. They see all these photos that have never been published, and it was guaranteed that you would find one of your heroes up on that wall. It's an awe-inspiring experience."

Glen and Markéta were similarly smitten and spent a fair amount of time checking out the photos, as well as the guitars, in the shop. As they prepared to leave, Lincoln offered, "If you ever want to do a show here, just let me know. And they said, 'How about tomorrow?'"

The concert director was not about to pass up this opportunity, even though Glen Phillips of the band Toad the Wet Sprocket was scheduled to play the next night. Lincoln checked in with Glen to make sure he would be agreeable to having a late show by the Swell Season after his concert. As it turned out, Glen was fine with clearing out right after his performance, as he needed to drive home to Santa Barbara, about two hours from Santa Monica, and relished the chance of getting an early start.

Lincoln quickly put together an email announcement for the Swell Season's 10:30 p.m. show, and it sold out in twenty minutes. On the night of the performance, Markéta came to Lincoln and explained that in addition to piano, she also played guitar on their show, but since they weren't on tour and were just in town to play at the Oscars, she hadn't brought one with her. No problem—Lincoln gestured toward the wall of guitars and told Markéta to take her pick. "She actually gravitated toward a really beautiful and expensive Martin guitar," he said. Marketa played the guitar and ended up taking it home with her.

The show was a smashing success, and the elation continued as Lincoln watched the duo, whom he had just presented in concert to 150 lucky people on the modest stage at McCabe's, perform their Oscar-nominated song live at the Kodak Theatre to over 3,000 movie stars and millions on national television. They won the Academy Award, making Markéta the youngest person to win in a nonacting category and Glen the first Irish-born person to win in the Best Original Song category.

The whole experience, undoubtedly one of the highlights of Lincoln's time at McCabe's, was made even more memorable when his phone rang the following morning. Markéta was on the line on her way to the airport. She wanted to thank Lincoln for providing them the opportunity to perform at McCabe's. "No one before—or since—ever called the next day to say thanks." The duo's success led to performances at large theaters and music festivals around the globe, yet they returned to play in the warm intimacy at McCabe's Guitar Shop in 2010 and 2012.

Just as the Swell Season happily landed in Lincoln's lap, another much less enjoyable situation presented itself in 2013, when Michelle Shocked, one of the day's cutting-edge alternative folk artists, was scheduled to play McCabe's. "Michelle played McCabe's dozens of times. When she first came out, she was the most exciting thing in folk music. She redefined folk for a lot of people," Lincoln said. So, when Michelle, who was booking her own appearances, contacted Lincoln to see about a stop at McCabe's on her 2013 tour, he immediately agreed.

A few days before the scheduled show, Lincoln became aware that Michelle had started her tour by making an impromptu speech against same-sex marriage at her first stop in San Francisco. This led some audience members to leave in protest and the club's management to end the show.

Lincoln was consequently inundated with requests from journalists looking for his plan of action and from ticket holders wondering if McCabe's still planned to proceed with the performance. Half expressed they would be disappointed if the show was canceled; the other half said they would be upset if the show proceeded.

Distraught, Lincoln decided to seek the advice of a legendary singer and songwriter who happened to be booked for the night following the scheduled Michelle Shocked concert.

Janis Ian played her first gig at the famous New York City folk club the Village Gate at the age of thirteen and then became an international star with the release of the controversial single "Society's Child" in 1967. When touring in Los Angeles in the '60s, she would play the Ash Grove, and as a result of her double Grammy-winning, multiplatinum album *Between the Lines* that included the mega-hit "At Seventeen," she headlined at the Troubadour and major concert halls.

Janis took a hiatus from music from 1983 to 1993 but lived in Santa Monica in the late 1980s, and McCabe's was her go-to place to get her guitars repaired.

When she re-emerged with her album *Breaking Silence*, Janis decided to play more intimate venues and made her debut at McCabe's in 1994. Janis recalled that her accompanists, percussionist Jim Brock and bassist Chad Watson, who were six foot, four inches tall and six foot, five inches tall, respectively, were set up on the floor, so she was the only one on the stage. Newcomer Gillian Welch opened the show.

Janis recalled the conversation with Lincoln about his Michelle Shocked dilemma: "He rightly wanted to be respectful of the gay community, but at the same time not get the club involved in a suit, and at the same time make sure that the club stayed true to its reputation, which was a listening room for all sorts of artists. We had a long discussion about 'where do you draw the line'—and that's a rough one."

As Lincoln continued to weigh his options, a call from a representative of the ACLU assured Lincoln that it was well in his purview to cancel under the circumstances—and they would back that decision.

After much consternation, Lincoln finally opted to pull the plug and canceled the event—as did nearly all of the other venues on the tour.

Janis Ian concluded, "I thought that the club handled it very gracefully," and she arrived for her own concert the next night. She continued to return in the years to come to play to packed houses. Oftentimes, her Hollywood friends came to see her shows, for which she was gratified. One night, when

Lily Tomlin arrived, "My tour manager met her in the alley and snuck her in the back and up the stairs."

In 2022, Janis decided to retire from touring and planned to take a farewell trek to many of her favorite venues—McCabe's "was definitely high on that list." Her three-night run was completely sold out. Thinking back on her experiences, she reflected, "If every major city had a club like McCabe's, the world would be a kinder, gentler place. I really mean that!"

In addition to presenting legendary artists such as Janis Ian, Lincoln was quick to invite newcomers like singer/songwriter Justin Townes Earle, banjo player Abigail Washburn, the string band the Carolina Chocolate Drops, and vocalist Aoife O'Donovan, who first played McCabe's with the contemporary bluegrass band Crooked Still in 2009. Aoife returned in 2011 with the alternative country band Ollabelle, filling in for singer Amy Helm. She recalled, "I was fascinated by McCabe's because I knew it was a guitar store, and I loved the idea of playing surrounded by guitars. I remember walking in and saying, 'This place is heaven.'"

Opposite: Janis Ian. *Photo by Camila Wilson.*

Right: Aoife O'Donovan's Listening Party. *Image provided by Aoife O'Donovan.*

Once Aoife went solo, she chose McCabe's as the place to workshop some of the songs she was considering for her second album, *The Magic Hour*. When some of the performances showed up on YouTube, Aoife was convinced the songs should be included and referenced the videos as she recorded the songs for the album. "I really wanted to capture that vibe," she said.

Then when Aoife was looking for a venue for a listening party for her 2024 double Grammy-nominated recording, *All My Friends*, she immediately thought of McCabe's. "I wanted to do a special event in L.A. I didn't want it to have any pretense or be industry-ish. I just wanted it to be a comfortable room that would sound great and feel very unique while I was unveiling my new project. There was something about the magic of McCabe's."

While many musicians aspired to play McCabe's, they often had to pay their dues at other venues while awaiting the moment they could take guitar shop's stage. Kenneth Pattengale grew up in Los Angeles and first attended a concert at McCabe's in 2006 to see Chris Smither: "A college friend turned me onto his records, and we went together. I remember the anticipation that accompanied waiting in line down Pico Boulevard. They only seat less than two hundred people, but somehow, it felt as electric as going into the Palladium amongst four thousand a decade earlier to see Rage Against the Machine."

While honing his skills as a singer, songwriter, and guitarist, Kenneth met Joey Ryan, who was following a similar path:

> *We came out of a different music scene in Los Angeles based around Hotel Cafe. That's where we met. That's where we had both been, largely developing our solo acts. You would book gigs on your own and sell tickets to your hour, but there would be five or six shows every evening back to back. The environment was very conducive to making friends and supporters of one another. At that time, we'd regularly visit multiple times a week just to socialize.*

It wasn't long before Kenneth and Joey started playing as a duo, and once they had sufficient material, they aspired to make their debut in 2011 at McCabe's Guitar Shop. Kenneth said:

> *When we decided to try a show at McCabe's, it was at a moment where were we felt confident to break away from our home turf, be able to sell enough tickets, and anchor an evening that was all our own. We both were aware of the venue's importance to various L.A. folk music eras, but neither of us really had a personal connection to it. It felt like an ambitious and significant jump out of the Hotel Cafe.*
>
> *Joey was living with his girlfriend (who would become his wife and mother to his kids) in Beachwood Canyon and I with my parents in Eagle Rock. I remember driving to his apartment because we wanted to drive to the show together. We drove surface streets from Hollywood to Santa Monica. I remember thinking on the drive there that we would see one hundred–plus people in the audience, but despite that, it felt like the biggest event of the year. Certainly of our career. A sold-out night at McCabe's. In ways, that night represents the upward trajectory of our career, and despite much hard work ahead of us, this was the moment that it all started to become the thing it is today.*

The thing it became was the Milk Carton Kids. The duo released two albums that same year, and as quickly as they sold out their debut performance at McCabe's, they started playing much larger venues. Several more albums

Top: Joey Ryan (*left*) and Kenneth Pattengale (*right*) before they were the Milk Carton Kids. *Image provided by the Milk Carton Kids.*

Bottom: Beck returns to McCabe's. *Poster design by Koko Peterson.*

and Grammy and Americana Music Award nominations later, they became one of the foremost folk music duos of the new millennium. But they still recall the venue that launched their career with great admiration: "The room is like a portal into another dimension, one where the instruments on the wall make their own reverb, where the audience is one-of-a-kind, one where the sound is always excellent. McCabe's has been there because the people needed it and still need it. Simple as that."

Lincoln Myerson reflected on his desire to make McCabe's available to traditional musicians, like bluegrass titan Ralph Stanley and zydeco master C.J. Chenier, as well as unconventional artists, like the self-described all-American Jewish lesbian folksinger Phranc. "There are plenty of folk artists that are historically significant…that don't have big draws. That in no way diminished the desire for them to play McCabe's. They are ambassadors of the genre. We have to have them there. That legitimizes McCabe's as a folk club."

In 2018, in recognition of McCabe's Guitar Shop's sixtieth anniversary, Lincoln put together a series of special benefit concerts, including shows by many the venues most honored performing artists.

An invitation was sent to Beck David Hansen (also known as Beck), who spent many of his days as a young musician growing up in Los Angeles at the shop. After a move to New York City, Beck returned to Los Angeles in the early 1990s and famously shared a bill on the McCabe's stage with Liz Phair in 1992.

Beck's ubiquitous single "Loser" and breakthrough album *Odelay* found him soon playing at major concert halls, festivals, and arenas around the world. Still, Lincoln remained hopeful that Beck would accept the invitation—and a year after it was extended, Beck accepted, performing on January 11, 2019.

The concert was one of the final acts of McCabe's longest-tenured concert director, and soon after, Lincoln got married, left the "best job I've ever had," and moved to New Zealand, handing the concert director reins to Koko Peterson and Brian Campos Rodriguez.

29
KEEP YOUR DISTANCE

Koko Peterson had a great respect for the history of McCabe's and understood the high esteem in which it was held by the artists who took its stage and the audiences who had occupied its seats for the past half century. However, Koko and her associate concert director, Brian Rodriguez, were champing at the bit to shake things up. "We went out and tried to bring a younger voice to McCabe's," Koko said. They envisioned outdoor pop-up music performances, Indian music concerts, and ukulele festivals developed with community partnerships, and they excitedly shared with each other YouTube videos of new artists they thought could bring a whole new dimension to the McCabe's stage.

Then, just as they were getting in high gear, the COVID pandemic put a wet blanket on their plans in March 2020. Brian left to pursue his own music career, but Koko remained and faced the challenge of being a concert director in a time when live performance venues were shuttered.

The impact of the COVID pandemic caused another significant change to McCabe's Guitar Shop: Bob and Espie Riskin decided to retire. They each had pre-existing conditions that made them more vulnerable to the effects of coronavirus.

Bob and Espie had become the sole owners of McCabe's Guitar Shop when Gerry McCabe, in order to concentrate on his furniture making endeavors, had sold his interest in McCabe's in 1986. Walter Camp, who had departed in 1970, retained a financial stake in the business until he passed away in 2016. At that point, his widow returned his shares to Bob

Riskin in exchange for having Walter's portrait hung permanently on the wall of the store. Bob and Espie also personally own the property where the shop has operated since 1972, which is likely a significant factor in McCabe's longevity. Their dedication to ensuring McCabe's kept its doors open was made evident when they decided to sell the Oscar statuette Bob's father, Robert Riskin, had won at the 1934 Academy Awards for his screenplay for *It Happened One Night* to pay off some bills. (Bob's mother was the acclaimed film actor Fay Wray, well known for her role as Ann Darrow in the 1933 film *King Kong*.)

Bob and Espie knew the day would come when they would have to retire—they just didn't know it would come as soon as it did. They already had a succession plan, and they put it in place. Their daughter Nora and her husband, Walt McGraw, would manage the store. While Walt and Nora had already been driving down from their home in Washington state more frequently to help the Riskins manage the guitar shop, the idea of taking on the day-to-day hands-on responsibilities took them a bit by surprise—but they readily agreed.

Normally, taking on the management of a business with a stellar reputation as a guitar store, repair shop, music school, and concert venue would have been—if not a walk in the park—at least a fairly easy road to navigate. However, these were far from normal times, and like every other organization in the world, Nora and Walt needed to discover new ways to stay in business until the shutdown order was lifted.

When the *Los Angeles Times* ran a story with a headline that included the words "McCabe's Guitar Shop Owners are Retiring," many readers, who had come to expect bad news in those dark days, immediately assumed the worst—that the shop was closing, and the concert series was over for good. As word spread on social media sites, McCabe's started receiving online sympathy cards and even had some flowers delivered to the store. The false alarm and the outpouring of support proved to cement the fact that McCabe's Guitar Shop had a special place in the hearts of the extended music community.

A follow-up article in *Variety* clarified that McCabe's was not closing, simply passing on day-to-day management responsibilities to Walt and Nora.

Meanwhile, Koko Peterson was trying to find a way to keep the McCabe's audience engaged with a concert venue that was closed to visitors.

The answer came when the City of Santa Monica began seeking proposals from organizations to develop a pilot project that would serve to jump-start the return to in-person live music shows. Realizing that this was exactly the kind of program Koko had hoped to implement at McCabe's, she wrote and submitted a proposal for a series of four free outdoor concerts that would feature a diverse mix of family-friendly, Southern California–based musicians titled "Americana in the Park." Koko's plan was awarded the grant funds, and she got to work booking the lineup, picking the park, designing the logo, arranging for food trucks, and taking care of other details.

The series premiered in the fall of 2021, providing artists and audiences an opportunity to enjoy live performances after an eighteen-month-long drought. It also reinforced just how valuable a cultural player McCabe's had been in Southern California, especially when the series closed with a performance by percussionist Joachim Cooder, accompanied by his father Ry Cooder, who honed his guitar chops at the shop six decades earlier. The success of the pilot project resulted in "Americana in the Park" becoming an annual fall event.

The project was administered with the guidance of the organization Community Arts Resources, whose mission—to design public spaces in which performing and visual arts, cultures, communities, and civic life collide—basically described what Koko envisioned for McCabe's future. As it turned out, the organization was searching for a production director, and with McCabe's indoor concerts still on hold, Koko applied and was hired.

Joachim Cooder (*left*) and Ry Cooder (*right*) perform at McCabe's first "Americana in the Park" series of outdoor concerts in 2021. *Photo by Gary Glade.*

Facing the challenge of relaunching the live concert series in a world that was just emerging from a time in which music fans were still concerned about the safety of attending indoor public gatherings, McCabe's was now in need of a new director who would understand the high esteem in which the venue was held by both artists and audiences, as well as the unique challenges of presenting performances in a venue that was a guitar shop by day and a show place by night. They didn't have to look very far.

While he says he "drew the short straw" as McCabe's looked around for a new concert director, Wayne Griffith, who had walked into the shop fifty years earlier as a young teen, started working the concerts in exchange for banjo lessons, and gone on to become the chief sound engineer for decades, was up for the challenge. He quickly got to work lining up legacy artists who'd had a home at McCabe's for over half a century, offering opportunities for up-and-comers, and making a commitment to feature bluegrass on a regular basis.

The series finally emerged from the pandemic shutdown in February 2022 with a performance by Carsie Blanton to a face-masked audience. Carsie's self-described mix of "American popular songs from folk and swing to pop-punk protest anthems inspired by artist-activists from Nina Simone to Woody Guthrie" boldly announced that the "Live at McCabe's Guitar Shop" concerts were back.

30
LIVING LEGACY

Steven Weiss became aware of McCabe's as a high school student in Cumberland, Maryland, when he read the article in the August 16, 1984 issue of *Rolling Stone* magazine "Guitar Stars Jam Club." The article was about the farewell concert for Nancy Covey. "I became a fan," he said. "After graduating from college in 1991, I visited California for the first time and made a stop at McCabe's."

Steve ultimately became the curator of the Southern Folklife Collection at the University of North Carolina (UNC), which was established when UNC purchased the John Edwards Memorial Collection (JEMC) and combined it with university's North Carolina Folk Archives. The JEMC was established in the early 1960s and was housed in an office at UCLA's Folklore and Mythology Department. During the JEMC's time in Los Angeles, many students, faculty, folklorists, and collectors were involved with the collection, including folklorist Ed Kahn, the very same Ed Kahn whom Gerald McCabe had hired to sell books and records when he started the guitar shop.

Bob Clark, a UNC alumnus and friend of the Southern Folklife Collection, introduced Steve Weiss to his guitar teacher at McCabe's, Kit Alderson. Kit, who had long been an advocate for the preservation of the McCabe's history, told him that nearly every concert at McCabe's had been recorded.

Throughout the years, Bob Riskin, who spent long days in the shop during the day, typically did not stay for the concerts, which he saw as the primary avenue for marketing the retail store. He explained why he asked for the performances to be recorded: "I insisted that they do it because I wanted to be sure they were pitching the store. They were supposed to say, 'We have a deal this week on ukuleles or Martin guitars.'"

The result was that well over two thousand live recordings were made on open-reel audio tape, audiocassette, Digital Audio Tape, and compact disc, along with many concert videos. When Steve heard about this treasure trove, he got in touch with Bob Riskin to start a conversation about the disposition of the recordings, and Bob agreed to donate them to the Southern Folklife Collection.

Steven finally saw his first concert at McCabe's in 2017. It was that Eric Andersen concert that Joni Mitchell attended around the time of the birth of the "Joni jams," and Steven was sitting just a few rows behind one of his folk music heroes.

Kit Alderson, who has been teaching at McCabe's since 1969 and who has tirelessly helped document McCabe's legacy, noted, "This all happened because of a fortunate combination of things, including Bob Clark's connection with Steve, my own stubborn attempts at preserving the tapes, Steve Weiss's polite and helpful personality, and Bob Riskin's common sense in accepting Steve's offer to preserve the tapes for posterity. The tapes are irreplaceable documents."

In assessing the collection, Steven reflected, "McCabe's is a national treasure, a unique place where listeners can experience the best in roots music in an intimate setting. Spanning decades, the collection is a who's who of roots music...[and] documents the history of the music, including the development of scenes, styles, artists, and songwriters. McCabe's concerts also speak to Los Angeles as a major node in our nation's musical culture."

In 2018, Bob Riskin was honored with a "Best of the West" Award from Folk Alliance Region–West that recognizes individuals who have maintained an enduring presence in the folk and acoustic music scene in the West and who continue to inspire others by embodying folk values and traditions. In 2024, Walt McGraw was on hand to receive a Lifetime Achievement Award from Folk Alliance International on behalf of McCabe's.

McCabe's ability to survive the ups and downs of the economy, the highs and lows of the concert industry, big box stores, online guitar sales, and even the COVID pandemic was summed up by music journalist Robert Hilburn, who wrote about music for the *Los Angeles Times* for many years: "Certainly the purity of the vision of the owners and people like Bobby [Kimmel] mattered because audiences learned to trust their taste. McCabe's booked musicians of merit, not just temporary hitmakers. Thus, many people headed to the club, I'm sure, just because they wanted a nice, warm evening of music—

without even knowing who was playing there on a particular night. The importance of that trust can't be overstated."

For singer/songwriter Tom Paxton, who gained international acclaim with songs such as "Ramblin' Boy" and "The Last Thing on My Mind," McCabe's has been his go-to stage in Los Angeles since the 1970s: "Always one of my favorite gigs....I love the audience there...the closeness, the intimacy of it....I'm practically in their laps when I'm singing. They have always been fantastically accepting of what I do."

Canadian singer/songwriter and guitarist Bruce Cockburn, who has been sharing his songs such as "Wondering Where the Lions Are" and "If I Had a Rocket Launcher" at McCabe's since 1984, can't explain the venue's longevity but is pleased it remains viable. "There are no record stores or as many quirky guitar stores that there used to be—and McCabe's is one of those—and how they've managed to hold on...I have no idea."

While hundreds of musicians have waxed poetic about McCabe's Guitar Shop, it's likely Wesley Stace is the most enthusiastic:

> *All I've wanted to do was to put out records and play at McCabe's, and miraculously, thirty-five years later, I've still got it! For some who play in larger theaters, that may seem a very limited ambition. But to me, it's just the best it could be. I have often joked that if I had been really, really rich, my entire tours would take place at McCabe's, and I would pay the airfare for audiences around the country so people could see me where I knew I'd be really f—ing good. You can't find anyone who loves it more than I do.*

Taj Mahal summarized the factors for McCabe's ability to stay afloat like this: "It was about the music. It was a place you could hang out and jam. You were allowed to take the instruments down and play them. It's really organic, the vibe was good there, man, and you had some conscientious people who looked out for the bottom line, and that's why they're still there."

EPILOGUE

By Walt McGraw, owner (2018–Present), McCabe's Guitar Shop

Bob Riskin—my father-in-law and the longtime steward of this fine circus—is on the record stating that running McCabe's is the neatest job in the world.

I believe him.

And so do a lot of people who've walked through these doors.

I was there in 2018, when Bob received the "Best of the West" Award from the Folk Alliance Region-West. Jackson Browne was there, too, smiling like he knew something the rest of us didn't. Bob and Espie introduced me to him as McCabe's "heir apparent." Jackson put a hand on my shoulder and said, "So, you realize how important this is?"

No pressure. Just the weight of six decades, twenty thousand concerts, and the hopes of many a singer who has graced—or dreamed of—our stage.

Being handed the torch of McCabe's legacy comes with strings attached—pun intended. But not just guitar strings. They're names. Faces. Voices. Communities. Without them, McCabe's wouldn't be McCabe's. In fact, it wouldn't be here at all.

As our sixtieth anniversary drew near, our finances were not in good shape. Enter Lincoln, our concert director, with a plan—and a Rolodex the size of a Dobro. What followed was a lineup that read like the liner notes of every record that ever mattered: Richard Thompson, Dave Alvin, Peter Case, Henry Rollins, Shelby Lynne, Tom Paxton, Inara George, Jackshit, Beck, and, yes, Jackson Browne.

They played benefit concerts. The community showed up. The music spoke. And the lights stayed on.

That's love. That's legacy. That's McCabe's.

So, here's to all our unsung heroes and, most of all, to those who sing.

BIBLIOGRAPHY

Books and Articles

Ankeny, Jason. "Rosanne Cash." AllMusic. www.allmusic.com.

———. "T Bone Burnett." AllMusic. www.allmusic.com.

Barnett, Sherry Rayn. *Eye of the Music*. Genius Book Publishing, 2020. www.sherrybarnettphotography.com/book.

Bing, Andy. "Norman Blake: An Appreciation." Hudson Valley Bluegrass Association. January 13, 2022. www.hvbluegrass.org.

Breedlove, Larry. "Shaping the Taylor Aesthetic." *Wood & Steel*, no. 79 (Spring/Summer 2014): 14. www.taylorguitars.com.

Ceriotti, Bruno. "The Rising Sons." *Bruno Ceriotti, Rock Historian*. www.brunoceriotti.weebly.com.

Crommelin, Richard. "Gerald McCabe Dies at 82; Founder of Folk Music Venue McCabe's Guitar Shop." *Los Angeles Times*, January 22, 2010. www.latimes.com.

Deming, Mark. "Steve Goodman." AllMusic. www.allmusic.com.

———. "Tom Rush." AllMusic. www.allmusic.com.

Dudley, Art. "Tony Rice and His Holy Grail Martin D-28." *Fretboard Journal*, no. 5 (Spring 2007). www.fretboardjournal.com.

Erlewine, Steven Thomas. "John Hiatt." AllMusic. www.allmusic.com.

Everett, Todd. "Rosanne Cash." *Variety*, July 22, 1996. www.variety.com.

Finkel, Bruria. "Pico Place: Goats Gulch." *Santa Monica Conservancy News* 2, no. 3 (July 2004): 6. www.smconservancy.org.

Fong-Torres, Ben. "Linda Ronstadt: Heartbreak on Wheels." *Rolling Stone*, March 27, 1975. www.ronstadt-linda.com.

Gallo, Phil. "A Half Century of Musical Influence." *Variety*, September 29, 2008. www.variety.com.

Gilmore, Mikal. "Unlikely Folk Greats Shine at McCabe's." *Los Angeles Herald-Examiner*, July 2, 1984. www.elviscostellofans.com.

Gluckin, Tzvi. "Forgotten Heroes: Clarence White." *Premier Guitar*, August 6, 2020. www.premierguitar.com.

Hongo, Garrett. "Keb' Mo' and the Resonator Guitar." *Harvard Review*, February 8, 2022. www.harvardreview.org.

Huey, Steve. "Henry Rollins." AllMusic. www.allmusic.com.

———. "Lucinda Williams." AllMusic. www.allmusic.com.

Kubernik, Harvey. "Legacy Recordings Celebrates Guitarist Michael Bloomfield with *From His Head to His Heart to His Hands* 3CD/1DVD Box Set." *Cave Hollywood*, February 13, 2014. www.cavehollywood.com.

Levy, Adam. "Still and All: Richard Thompson Looks Forward and Back." *Fretboard Journal*, April 2016. www.fretboardjournal.com.

Lewis, Randy. "McCabe's Concert Booker, Grammy-Winning Producer John Chelew, Dies at 65." *Los Angeles Times*, December 29, 2016. www.latimes.com.

McCabe's Guitar Shop: The First Fifty Years, 1958–2008. McCabe's Guitar Shop, 2008.

McEuen, John. *The Life I've Picked.* Chicago Review Press, 2018. www.chicagoreviewpress.com.

Mirkin, Steven. "McCabe's 50th Anniversary: A Living History of Music." *Variety*, October 3, 2008. www.variety.com.

O'Connor, Mark. *Crossing Bridges.* Mark O'Connor Musik International, 2023. www.markoconnor.com.

Park, Andrew. "One Guitar's Journey from Clarence White to Tony Rice to Billy Strings and Beyond." *No Depression*, February 16, 2024. www.nodepression.com.

Perlmutter, Adam. "Legendary McCabe's Guitar Shop Is a Mecca for LA Guitarists." *Acoustic Guitar*, July 27, 2016. www.acousticguitar.com.

Riskin, Robert. *Celebrating 20 Years at McCabe's 1979 Calendar and Scrapbook.* N.p., 1979.

Roberts, Randall. "After Five Decades, McCabe's Guitar Shop Owners are Retiring, Citing Coronavirus Crisis." *Los Angeles Times*, June 7, 2020. www.latimes.com.

Roland, Terry. "Eric Andersen at McCabe's: A Bittersweet Reunion with Joni Mitchell." *No Depression*, June 28, 2017. www.nodepression.com.

Simmons, Michael. "A Half Century of McCabe's Guitar Shop." *LA Weekly*, October 12, 2008. www.laweekly.com.

Smith, Jim. "Norman Blake Live at McCabe's." AllMusic. www.allmusic.com.

Strauss, Duncan. "The Book on John Chelew." *Los Angeles Times*, July 26, 1987. www.latimes.com.

Willman, Chris. "Andersen Stages Folk at McCabe's." *Los Angeles Times*, May 13, 1991. www.latimes.com.

———. "Michelle Shocked Announces McCabe's Appearance." *Hollywood Reporter*, March 22, 2013. www.hollywoodreporter.com.

———. "No, McCabe's in Santa Monica Is Not Closing—So Hold Off on the Flowers." *Variety*, June 8, 2020. www.variety.com.

Wood, John. "Remembering the Lovely, Talented Marcia Berman." *Topanga New Times*, April 3, 2025. www.topanganewtimes.com.

Zack, Ian. *Say No to the Devil: The Life and Musical Genius of Rev. Gary Davis*. University of Chicago Press, 2015. www.press.uchicago.edu.

Audio/Video

banjomaniacs. "19—Pat Cloud—Banjo Meltdown 1992." YouTube. Posted January 26, 2017. www.youtube.com.

Calamar, Gary. "McCabe's 50th Anniversary." KCRW. Aired September 28, 2008. www.kcrw.com.

Country Music Hall of Fame and Museum. "Ry Cooder | Interview, 2014." www.watch.countrymusichalloffame.org.

Folk Alliance International. "Lifetime Achievement Award | McCabe's Guitar Shop." Facebook. Posted June 5, 2024. www.facebook.com.

KCRW. "McCabe's at 50." Aired November 27, 2008. www.kcrw.com.

Living Legacies Productions. "A Celebration of Marcia Berman." YouTube. Posted November 5, 2013. www.youtube.com.

Mike Bloomfield-Topic. "I'm With You Always." YouTube. Posted March 11, 2019. www.youtube.com.

Norman Blake. "Nine Pound Hammer (Live)." YouTube. Posted November 12, 2018. www.youtube.com.

Omnivore Recordings. "John Wesley Harding 'Wreck on the Highway' with Bruce Springsteen Official Video." YouTube. Posted April 17, 2018. www.youtube.com.

Parnes, Fred, dir. *Peter Case: A Million Miles Away*. Passport 2020, 2023. YouTube Movies & TV. www.youtube.com.

Tankard1990. "Townes Van Zandt—Live at McCabe's—01—'Pueblo Waltz." YouTube. Posted December 29, 2012. www.youtube.com.

Wayne Griffith. "Elvis Costello—'So You Want to Be a Rock 'n' Roll Star'—Live at McCabe's, 1984." YouTube. Posted October 14, 2020. www.youtube.com.

Websites

Arlo Guthrie. www.gut3.me.
Bluegrass Music Hall of Fame and Museum. "Norman Lee Blake." www.bluegrasshall.org.
Cave Hollywood. "Harvey Kubernik." www.cavehollywood.com.
Chris Smither. "Biography." www.smither.com.
Dave Alvin. www.davealvin.net.
David Lindley. www.davidlindley.com.
Esalen Institute. www.esalen.org.
Fran Banish. www.franbanish.com.
Fred Sokolow Music. www.sokolowmusic.com.
George Winston. www.georgewinston.com.
Jackson Browne. www.jacksonbrowne.com.
Janis Ian. www.janisian.com.
Jerry Garcia's Middle Finger. "The Birth of the Great American Music Band." November 17, 2010. www.jgmf.blogspot.com.
Joni Mitchell. www.jonimitchell.com.
Joni Mitchell Fans. Post by Eric Andersen. Facebook. August 15, 2023. www.facebook.com.
Justin Roberts. www.justinrobertsmusic.com.
Larry Campbell. www.larrycampbellmusic.net.
Los Lobos. www.loslobos.org.
Loudon Wainwright III. www.lw3.com.
Mark O'Connor. www.markoconnor.com.
McCabe's Guitar Shop. "Our Back Room." www.mccabes.com.
Michael Bloomfield. www.michaelbloomfield.com.
Milk Carton Kids. www.themilkcartonkids.com.
Miller, Dan. "A Biography of Doc Watson." Edited by Steve Carr. www.docsguitar.com.
Music Connection. "Far-West Conference Honors '2018 Best of the West' Performer Wendy Waldman and Ambassador McCabe's Guitar Shop Owned by Bob Riskin." June 4, 2018. www.musicconnection.com.
Nels Cline. www.nelscline.com.
Pat Cloud. www.patcloud.com.
Peter Case. www.petercase.com.
Peter Rowan. www.peter-rowan.com.
Ramblin' Jack Elliott. www.ramblinjackelliott.com.
Richard Thompson. www.richardthompson-music.com.
Sam Bush. www.sambush.com.

Self Portrait Gospel. "The Rick Ruskin Interview." June 1, 2024. www.theselfportraitgospel.com.
Simian Ridge Guitars Repair/Simian Ridge Guitars. www.simianridge.co.nz.
Sing Out! www.singout.org.
Smithsonian Folkways Recordings. "Artist Spotlight: Elizabeth Cotten." www.folkways.si.edu.
———. "Mission and History." www.folkways.si.edu.
Steve Wynn. www.stevewynn.net.
Stoned Soul Picnic: A Celebration of the Music of Laura Nyro. www.stonedsoulpicnic.com.
Taj Mahal. www.tajblues.com.
Tony Trischka. www.tonytrischka.com.
Toulouse Engelhardt. www.toulouse-music.com.
University of North Carolina Libraries. "McCabe's Guitar Shop Collection, 1967–2013." Southern Folklife Collection. www.finding-aids.lib.unc.edu.
Wesley Stace. www.wesleystace.com.

ABOUT THE AUTHOR

Photo by Therese Lesser.

Peter Alan Lesser was a concert director in Upstate New York for over thirty years. He presented performances at the Java Jive Coffee House, Troy Savings Bank Music Hall, and Empire State Plaza Performing Arts Center before moving to Santa Monica, just a couple of miles from McCabe's Guitar Shop, where he now lives with his wife, Therese.